D1179810

Light on Saint John

MAHARAJ CHARAN SINGH AND AUDIENCE AT DERA INTERNATIONAL GUEST HOUSE MEETING HALL.

Light on Saint John

"In the beginning was the Word, and the
Word was with God, and the Word was God."

MAHARAJ CHARAN SINGH

RADHA SOAMI SATSANG BEAS
PUNJAB, INDIA

Published by
S. L. Sondhi, Secretary
Radha Soami Satsang Beas
P.O. Dera Baba Jaimal Singh
Dist. Amritsar 143 204
Punjab, India

First edition	1967	3,000 copies
Second edition (revised and enlarged)	1971	3,000 copies
Third edition	1974	5,000 copies
Fourth edition	1978	5,000 copies
Fifth edition (enlarged)	1985	10,000 copies

Printed at India Offset Press, A-1 Mayapuri Ind. Area, Ring Road,
New Delhi 110064

CONTENTS

PREFACE TO THE FIFTH EDITION

THIS BOOK was originally published under the title *Saint John the Great Mystic*. Since then the Master, Maharaj Charan Singh, during the English meetings he holds at the Dera for satsangis from abroad, and during his foreign satsang tours, has given more discourses on the Gospel according to Saint John, stressing different points at different times. As the audiences at these meetings were familiar with Sant Mat, 'the teachings of the Saints', the Master did not go into much detail, but simply tried to bring out the similarity in the teachings of all true Saints. He therefore did not dwell on the narratives but only on the words of Christ that are relevant to the teachings. If the reader is interested in knowing more about Sant Mat, he may find a detailed explanation in our other books, a list of which is included herein.

The present volume, presented under the new title *Light on Saint John*, was compiled and typed by Arnold Howard of the United States from tape recordings of Maharaj Ji's talks (including questions and answers) and from material published in the previous edition. We are extremely grateful to him for undertaking this laborious task and sending us an elegantly finished manuscript. Since the material is taken from recordings, Maharaj Ji has personally edited the entire manuscript in order to make the book more comprehensive. Additional information is given wherever required.

We are thankful to Alexander R. Tobin of the United States and to V. K. Sethi and Professor J. M. L. Bhatnagar for going through the entire manuscript and making valuable suggestions, and to Louise Hilger for checking the manuscript and typing the final copy. Bruce and Anthea Becker of the United States have prepared the index and arranged the references, a dedicated labor of love appreciated by all. We also thank Wayne and Miriam Caravella for preparation of the press copy, design, and production.

S. L. Sondhi
Secretary

Radha Soami Satsang Beas
Punjab, India
July 1985

PREFACE TO THE SECOND EDITON

DURING his 1970 tour of the Continent and the United States, Maharaj Ji gave many discourses from the Bible, which were meticulously taped and preserved. Miss Margrith Yenni of Italy has critically gone through the first edition of this book and has made numerous useful suggestions. Mr. Andrew Rawlinson of the United Kingdom has fully drawn on all this material, including the transcripts of the tapes, and has very ably edited, revised, and enlarged the first edition in the light thereof. This was indeed a stupendous task but his loving devotion and dedication to the Master proved equal to it, and the result is indeed most gratifying. We earnestly hope that seekers of Truth will find in this second edition the rare "food" they have been longing for, which will entirely appease their hunger. We are greatly beholden to both Miss Yenni and Mr. Rawlinson for their labor of love in the service of the Master.

K. L. Khanna
Secretary

Radha Soami Satsang Beas
Punjab, India
June 15, 1971

PREFACE TO THE FIRST EDITON

DURING the last season a large number of foreigners from nearly thirty countries visited the Colony. In the group meetings held every evening for a couple of hours, the Bible had the pride of place as Maharaj Ji explained the teachings of the Mystics from the perspective of this great book. He delivered a series of lectures on Saint John, lucidly and succinctly bringing out the universal teachings of Jesus Christ.

All messengers of God have the same message to give and the same one Truth to teach. Their message has always been the same one of love, compassion, and humility. They all enjoin us to go to the kernel and leave aside the shell. They come to unite and not to divide. They emphasize the unity of God and brotherhood of man. This one Being is the goal of all, and the faculty that comprehends Him is the same in all.

These lectures were taken down verbatim in shorthand and are being printed for the benefit of seekers and satsangis. The reader will doubtless find the rare jewels of Christ's teachings, in all their splendor and glory, displayed in these pages. The world of Mystics is truly one and it transcends caste, creed, color, and country. Their heritage is one and indivisible.

Miss Louise Hilger did the entire note-taking and typing of the manuscript, and Professor M. S. Bhatnagar has seen the book through the press. We greatly appreciate their labor of love in the service of the beloved Master.

K. L. Khanna
Secretary

Radha Soami Satsang Beas
Punjab, India
June 1, 1967

INTRODUCTION

SINCE MOST of you have a Christian background, I shall try to explain the teaching of all the Saints in the light of the Bible, for their teachings exactly coincide with those contained in the Bible, if rightly understood. Rulers, priests, and politicians always try to suppress the truth. So it was in the time of Christ, and even more so in that of the Old Testament. The truth had to be spoken in veiled language so that it could be understood only by the real seekers.

Every word spoken by Christ has a deep mystic meaning. While I am no authority on the Bible, when I first read it I was amazed to find that even the little that has been handed down to us as the teachings of Jesus substantially tallies with the teachings of all true Saints, regardless of their color, religion, country, or time. The truth is always the same, but after the departure of the spiritual teacher his message is forgotten and is given the shape of organized religion with rites, ceremonies, and dogmas. Eventually all emphasis is placed on these rites and ceremonies, and the real truth is lost.

As you all know, Christ had very little time to share his teachings with the masses; he lived for only a very short period. And then, he could not stay in one place— he moved from one place to another. He was hunted by the priests of the organized religions, who are always frightened of the popularity of the Mystics, because that generally affects their income. Unfortunately for posterity, the Bible was not written by Christ himself, nor were notes taken at the time that he spoke so that we could have his teachings verbatim. They were passed on by word of mouth, and that portion which was remembered was recorded many years after his crucifixion.

Yesterday Professor Bhatnagar read to you from Kabir—and in this modern age you are all intellectual people—with your best effort, if you try to reproduce today what you heard from him only twenty-four hours ago, the result will hardly be 15 percent of what he said, and that will not be in the exact words of Professor Bhatnagar—it will be the gist of what he told you. Then, if you go and tell your friend, who has never heard Professor Bhatnagar, that this is what he said yesterday, and your friend tries to reproduce that on paper after just twenty-four hours, how much of what Professor said will be left? And if what is left is translated from one language to another language and then to a third language, perhaps only 5 percent of what Professor Bhatnagar said will be left. This is what happens after only twenty-four hours, and the Bible was written many years after the crucifixion. And then, Christ was addressing very simple people—some were fishermen, some farmers, some were carpenters, and so on. They were not intellectuals, men of letters. Accordingly, the precise words and statements of Christ are not with us today, though the writers of the Gospels did capture much of his meaning.

The Gospels themselves are "according" to Saint John, "according" to Saint Matthew. They were not even written by people who knew Christ personally. Moreover, the Bible has gone through many translations and through the hands of many people who wanted to suppress whatever did not suit their own selfish ends. It is a wonder that we still have so much of the mystical truth left. By translation from one language to another, many spiritual and mystical truths have been lost to the Bible, because the scholars themselves had no *experience* of what they were trying to translate. They intellectually tried to translate the teachings of Christ, but as they had no experience of their own, they did not understand many things; and in "straightening" the language in the modern versions of the Bible, much of the depth and meaning has been lost. I would say that many things which they could not understand have been eliminated.

For example, I was reading *The Gospel According to Thomas,* a manuscript found in Egypt. The translator has given the original Coptic language on one page and his own translation on the opposite page, so that scholars can see whether or not he has done justice to the original. At one place is mentioned five trees which are eternal: "For you have five trees in Paradise which are unmoved in summer or in winter, and their leaves do not fall. Whoever knows them will not taste death."[1] It must be referring to the five Sounds and five regions frequently mentioned by Mystics; at least I could not find any other meaning. It is clearly written, but is nowhere found in the Bible, which suggests that much is missing from the Bible.

I have also compared parts of the King James version of the Bible with modern English versions, and there is a lot of difference. At many places the word *food* occurs in the King James version. Now, modern editors have replaced it with the word *meat*. First it was clearly written, "Thou shalt not kill." Now they have replaced it with, "You must not murder." *Murder* refers

---

1. *The Gospel According to Thomas.* trans. A. Guillaumont et al. (New York: Harper and Row, 1959), pp. 13–15.

to human beings only. A thousand years from now people will probably think Moses had said this—that is how adulteration starts. The scholars have "straightened" the English, but they have misinterpreted his teachings and misguided the people.

Fortunately, Jesus spoke in such simple language that his parables, which contained deep, hidden meanings, seemed meaningless to his contemporaries. As a result, they were not tampered with, and we still have these beautiful jewels in the Bible from which we can glean the mystical gist of his teachings and corroborate them with the teachings of Saints of ancient and of modern times. But one cannot read the Bible like a novel, nor can one read it like a legal document, interpreting every sentence, every period and comma, because many links are missing. It has to be studied with concentrated attention if we want to understand its true meaning.

Saints may come into this world at any time and in any country, yet their teachings are bound to be the same. The teachings of different Saints cannot themselves be different. Because the Lord is one, the way to realize Him must also be one, for He is within every one of us. We have to search for Him within ourselves, under the guidance of one who has himself realized Him within, as Christ did in his lifetime. Naturally there cannot be two or more paths leading to God; there can be only one. The rites and rituals of all religions are our own creation, but at the base of all of them is the same essence of Truth, Reality, and Spirituality.

Masters may take birth in any nation, race, or religion, but they all preach the same Truth. They come, not to condemn any religion nor to establish a new one, but to create in us a longing for that Reality; and they explain to us the method and means to realize it. They all have the same message to give, the same spiritual Truth to share with us. Christ, too, in this gospel, has referred to that Truth and has drawn our attention to the Father, the creative and sustaining Power within.

Different Mystics, at different times, have referred to that same Power by different names. Christ called it Word, Logos, Spirit, Name, Holy Ghost, and the Voice of God. Persian and Arabic Mystics have named it *Kalma, Bang-i-Asmani, Nada-i-Sultani, Ism-i-Azam, Sultan-Al-Azkar,* and many other names. Indian Mystics have called it *Akash Bani, Ram Nam, Ram Dhun, Nirmal Nad,* and, more generally, *Shabd,* or *Nam.*The Chinese called it *Tao.* This divine Power is also known by many other names.

All true Mystics point only towards that Reality by means of which the Lord created this universe. That same Reality is the Lord himself, who is the very foundation of all that is manifested and keeps the creation in existence. When we realize that Reality within our selves, we become whole and pure, and worthy of becoming one with the Lord.

After such Saints and Mystics leave the world, we deviate far from their real teachings and become entangled in rites, rituals, and ceremonies, which lead us outwards. Thus we arrest the real teachings in small, narrow compartments and give them the forms of religions, nations, and countries. Then we begin to quarrel with one another.

The path has always been the same. It has been taught by all Saints and it is also taught now, in modern times, to all true seekers and lovers of the Lord. That is why there is so much similarity between the teachings of the Bible and those of Persian, Indian, and other true

Mystics. The teachings are the same. The approach
may be different, our interpretations may be different,
but the teachings cannot be different. Christ's parables
had to suit the conditions that existed in that area at that
time; but today we cannot as effectively employ the
same parables, because conditions now are different.
People are perhaps more intellectual, and parables that
suited the conditions two thousand years ago may not
be able to satisfy the modern mind.

For example, somewhere in the Bible is written that
eagles (vultures) come wherever there is a carcass.[1]
Christ was explaining that whenever a Son of the Father
comes, devotees always flock around that Mystic to
imbibe his teachings. The example appears to be crude
and not in good taste, but I think Christ had no other
option, because that was the only way he could illus-
trate his teachings to those desert people. In a desert,
when there are dead bodies, vultures gather to eat the
carcasses. Those people understood what he was trying
to explain much better with this example than they
would have with any other. Saints have to explain their
teachings, keeping in view the background, the intellect, and the traditions in which the people in the audience have been brought up.

But still, many of the mystic parables and similes
that I read in the Bible are like those given by other
Mystics, and even their way of explaining is the same.
Christ refers to the key to the door of heaven,[2] and Guru
Nanak also refers to the same thing. I was reading a
book written by a missionary who even wrote to the

---

1. "For wheresoever the carcase is, there will the eagles be gathered
together" (Matt. 24:28).
2. "And I will give unto thee the keys of the kingdom of heaven" (Matt.
16:19).

extent that Guru Nanak seems to have borrowed all these ideas from Christ, because the ideas are similar. But historians do not understand that *whosoever walks on the same path and reaches the same goal will have the same things to explain*. There is no question of one borrowing from the other, because in the time of Guru Nanak, Christianity was hardly known in India. Hence the question of Guru Nanak having any contact with the missionaries or reading the Bible in any way does not arise.

If you go deep into the roots of Christ's teachings, you will find that his teachings are the same as the teachings of all other Saints, and in that light I will discuss Saint John with you.

1

In the beginning was the Word, and the Word
was with God, and the Word was God. *(1:1)*[1]

Before there was any creation at all, only the Lord
existed. He has created this whole universe through the
Word, and there is no difference between the Lord and
the Word, the Holy Spirit, the Holy Ghost, the Shabd,
the Nam or Name, or the divine Sound Current. The
Creator and the Creative Power are one and the same.
The "Word" cannot be written, it cannot be spoken, it
cannot be touched. It is not the physical eyes which see
it, nor the physical ears which hear it. It is within every
one of us.

Most religions take the spoken words for the real
Word of God, but they are not the Word of God. We
cannot trace the history of the Word, because it has
created the whole creation; but we can trace the history
of the words we read in the Bible, in the Koran, in the
Adi Granth, or in any other book. They can be written,
they can be spoken, they can be heard, they can be
seen; but that Word cannot be heard with these ears,
cannot be seen by these eyes, cannot be spoken by the
tongue.

The Word to which Christ refers has both Sound and
Light. Elsewhere in the Bible he alludes to the Light of

---

1. All biblical quotations are from the Authorized King James version of
the Bible.

the Word: "If therefore thine eye be single, thy whole body shall be full of light."[1] This means that we will be able to experience and enjoy the Light of that Word when we withdraw our consciousness to the eye center. He also indicates that we can enjoy the bliss of the Sound of that Word, when he says, "The wind bloweth where it listeth, and thou hearest the sound thereof, but canst not tell whence it cometh, and whither it goeth."[2] Here Christ is actually describing the Voice of God within and the effulgence of the Light which emanates from the Word of God. This will be described in detail further on.

The creation will perish, but the Creative Power, the Word, or Shabd, will not perish. That is God himself, His own projection. He has projected himself throughout the whole creation. The whole universe is being sustained by that Creative Power, which is also known as the Holy Spirit, the Holy Ghost, the divine Sound Current, the Nam, and by many other names. If the Lord would withdraw it, everything would come to an end.

The same was in the beginning with God. *(1:2)*

The Word was with God in the beginning, the Word is with God now, and the Word will always be with God. He alone is true, eternal, and unchangeable. Everything that we see in this world will perish, but the Word—that Power, that Shabd, Nam, or Holy Ghost—will never be destroyed; it will always remain the same.

---

1. *Matt. 6:22.*
2. *John 3:8.*

All things were made by him; and without him
was not any thing made that was made. *(1:3)*

This means that everything was created by Him.
Nothing was created except by Him; none else was
there to make anything. The Lord is everywhere and we
live and breathe in Him. God has created the universe
and everything in it through His own Word, Shabd,
Nam, Holy Ghost, or whatever name we may give to
this Power which is all love. There is nothing in existence that was not created by this Word of God and that
is not sustained by it.

In him was life; and the life was the light of men.
(1:4)

Before the creation, only He had life, because only
He existed. After the creation, He shared the same life
with His creation; we will find that same life in every
part of the creation. At the time of creation, the Lord, in
the form of Light, entered within all of us. That Light of
God is the life in every one of us.

The Light that we see within, with the inner or the
"single" eye, is the Light of our own soul. The moment
the Lord withdraws the soul from the body, the body
decomposes. The soul is of the same essence as the
Divine Light. It is a drop of that Divine Ocean and is
always shining within every one of us, irrespective of
caste or creed, country or religion.

This body is composed of five elements—earth,
water, fire, air, and ether. All these five elements are
antagonistic to one another. Earth is dissolved by water,
water is dried by fire, fire is consumed by air, and air is
absorbed by ether. But the soul in the body gives life to

these five elements and makes them compatible with one another. The moment the Lord withdraws the soul from the body, we die—and earth merges in earth, water merges in water, fire merges in fire, air in air, and ether in ether.

> And the light shineth in the darkness; and the
> darkness comprehended it not.   *(1:5)*

The soul gives life to everybody, and the soul—the Father himself—is a shining Light within every one of us, but we do not see that Light now. When we close our eyes we see only darkness within. Why do we not see that Light? Because in the process of creation, the soul, in its descent, became embedded and entangled with the mind to such an extent that the mind prevents the Light of the soul from shining through. This is because, having come from the Father to the level of creation, the soul has forgotten the Creator. And the mind, being attached to the creation and its sensual pleasures, has collected a lot of sins, or karmas, during many past lifetimes. This has clouded the mind to such an extent that it has become an impenetrable covering over the soul—a veil of darkness, which prevents us from enjoying or seeing the Light.

The veil of darkness is composed of the sins we have committed in our past births. That is why Christ says, "Repent ye: for the kingdom of heaven is at hand" and "the kingdom of God is within you."[1] The Father is not to be seen outside. He is within every one of us, but before we can see Him within we have to repent, in

---

1. *Matt. 3:2; Luke 17:21.*

order to remove that veil of darkness. Repent for what? Just after taking birth, a child has not done anything in this world to repent for, so why can he not see the Father within himself? Because he has done something in his past lives, so he has to repent for all the karmas he has been carrying from birth to birth.

In our body, the seat of the soul and mind knotted together is at the eye center. If we are able to still our mind at the eye center, as taught by a perfect Master, then we can see that Light within ourself. Actually there is nothing but Light within us, provided we are able to come back to the eye center. As is mentioned in the Bible, "The light of the body is the eye: if therefore thine eye be single, thy whole body shall be full of light; but if thine eye be evil, thy whole body shall be full of darkness."[1]

The Light which Christ is referring to here is at the eye center. But our mind is at the level of the senses and is attached to the creation, therefore we do not experience that Light and remain in the darkness of illusion. Having taken association of the mind, the soul is being pulled from the eye center to the senses; and as long as we are a slave of the senses, the veil of darkness between us and the Father cannot be eliminated. We are attached to worldly faces, to worldly objects, to sensual pleasures, and this attachment to the creation has become an obstruction between us and the Father.

Until the mind experiences the Light and is attached to the Sound it does not become pure. With the help of the Sound we know the direction of our "house" within, and with the help of the Light we can see within so we can travel the spiritual path. That is why Christ refers to

---

1. *Matt. 6:22–23.*

that Divine Light and Sound as the Voice of God, which ultimately gives us eternal life. Since the mind is fond of sensual pleasures, unless it gets a better pleasure than those of the senses, it refuses to leave them. And the better pleasure is that of experiencing the Divine Light and Voice of God within. It is so enchanting and so pulling that the mind, of itself, leaves the pleasure of the senses and comes back to its own source, Trikuti, the second spiritual region. This is where the obstruction is removed and the soul gets release from the clutches of the mind.

Saint John says: You cannot see the Light within you unless you are able to eliminate that veil of darkness— and how can you eliminate it? Only with the grace of the Father. Without His grace, you will never walk out of this darkness, you will never see the Creator who is within every one of us. And how do we obtain His grace, how do we come in contact with a Master? The Bible tells us:

> There was a man sent from God, whose name
> was John.   *(1:6)*

When the Father wants us to eliminate this veil of darkness and realize Him within ourselves, He sends somebody from His level to our level. At that time John the Baptist was sent from God. He was sent to initiate, or baptize, those who were ready during his lifetime, so they could remove the veil of darkness and see the Light and hear the Sound that would take them back to the Lord—which is the main purpose of human birth.

Saint John reveals that we can eliminate this veil of darkness and see the Light of the Lord within us only when, with His grace, we come in contact with someone who has come from the Father and who, after having come to our level, is also at the level of the Father. Otherwise, how can we worship Him whom we have never seen and whom we have never known since we have come to this creation? How can we love Him if we do not know what He looks like? So the necessity of the living Master arises. The Father sends His Sons to our level so that through them we also may reach the Father. If it were not so, there would be no link between us and the Father.

If I may say so, either we do not need a Master at all in order to worship the Lord, or if we need one, he has to be a living Master, because the relationship of the soul and the Father is that of love—we cannot love a person whom we have never seen. That is why Christ refers to this relationship of the soul with the Lord as that of father and son, also as that of bride and bridegroom, because in both these relationships it is the love that binds them. It is purely a bond of love. And if we love the Father, we go back to the level of the Father after death. The Father has so ordained that we can love Him only through His beloved Son who is living in this world when we are here.

We go where our attachments are, and if we are attached to the faces and objects of the creation, then we come back to the level of the creation after death. We love the creation because we see it, we live in it, we associate with its faces and objects, and possess them; so naturally we develop great affinity and attraction for these faces and objects. But this whole creation is to perish, so our attachment to the creation always keeps us tied down to the level of this perishable creation. Unless we love the Father and are attached to the Father, we cannot go back to the level of the Father.

How can we love someone whom we have never seen, whom we neither know nor have any idea of what he looks like? So the Father himself comes in the garb of His Son, to our level. He is, as Christ says, the "Word made flesh." So God, or the Word, dwells among us in the flesh, at our level. Being at our level, that "Word made flesh" is also at the level of the Father. Our attachment to the Word made flesh automatically detaches us from this creation and attaches us to the Father, because the Sons of the Father are actually waves of that Divine Ocean. Their relationship with the Father is that of the wave with the ocean. A wave in the ocean may seem to us as being different from the ocean, but it cannot be separated from the ocean—it always remains part and parcel of the ocean. So anything given to the wave is automatically merged with the ocean. That is why we need the association, company, and guidance of a living Master, so that this attachment to the Son may lead us back to the level of the Father. Because the Father is in heaven and we are in this creation and do not know whom we are loving, the Master is the link between us and the Father.

Christ said, "I and my Father are one."[1] He also mentions in the Bible, "He that loveth father or mother more than me is not worthy of me."[2] This means: When you become worthy of me, you become worthy of the Father; and unless you become me, you cannot become God. Since we have not seen the past Masters and we do not know what they look like, we cannot fall in love with them—we cannot become attached to them. We therefore need a living Master.

---

1. *John* 10:30.
2. *Matt.* 10:37.

The Bible says, John the Baptist was with God. One who is with God is no less than God. He came from God, and he and God are one and the same. A drop in the ocean is the ocean itself.

> The same came for a witness, to bear witness
> of the Light, that all men through him might
> believe. *(1:7)*

John the Baptist was sent to mankind by God so that those whom the Father wished to draw back to himself and who were ready for it might experience that Light— the Word—that the Lord has kept within every one of us. Every Saint, despite the fact that he is in the human form, sees the Light of God within himself, and it is only through the Saints that we can also see that Light. Saint John is explaining to us that the Saints, the Masters, come as a witness to the existence of the Light so that "all men through him might believe," that is, might experience that Light that God has kept within us. Without the Son of the Father, without John the Baptist, who was the Redeemer, or Master, *of that time,* the people *who were living then* could not remove that veil of ignorance, that darkness, from within themselves. It is only with the grace of the Father, through a perfect Master, that we are able to come out of this darkness.

> He was not that Light, but was sent to bear
> witness of that Light. *(1:8)*

This may sound contradictory, because first Saint John says that the Light is within every man, and now he says, "He was not that Light." It simply means that the flesh and blood, the body of man, is not the Light; it is the soul within that shines after all this darkness is removed. Saint John the Baptist, like all Masters of the past and present, was sent into this world in the garb of a human being so that he could enlighten mankind by bearing witness to that Light within. Flesh and blood is not the true form of any Saint—that is what is meant by saying that he was not that Light.

> That was the true Light, which lighteth every
> man that cometh into the world.   *(1:9)*

That inner Light, the Word, alone is the true Light. This worldly light will perish, but that true Light within every one of us will never perish. We need neither a wick nor wax nor anything from the outside to light it, and it is always shining within us whether we can see it or not. The Light of God is in His entire creation as long as the creation exists. The creation may perish when He so wills it, but the Light of God will never perish.

That Light is within "every man that cometh into the world." In fact, that Light *gives* us life. Without it we would not even exist. The Lord does not show partiality by putting it in one person and not putting it in another, nor by putting it in the followers of one religion and not in those of another. He has put that Light in all that He has created, within every one of us, irrespective of our status, creed, color, or nationality.

> He was in the world, and the world was made by
> him, and the world knew him not.   *(1:10)*

The Lord himself came to the level of His own creation in the garb of John the Baptist. He came as a man so that He could communicate with men, and His own creation never recognized that the Creator had come, because the Lord was in human form just like other men. People mistakenly take all Masters as ordinary human beings. They do not understand the significance of the perfect living Master, that though being here among us he is God incarnate.

After having separated from the Father, we are so lost in the love of this illusion that we forget even our Creator. And when the Father comes to our level as the Word made flesh, we do not even recognize him, because this whole world has become the be-all and end-all for us and we have become victims of the senses. Being at the level of the creation, we cannot know anything about the Creator who is beyond us; therefore, only a human being can teach a human being. Thus, unless the Father comes in the garb of a human being, we cannot communicate with Him, we cannot know Him. That is why He comes to our level—to tell us about Himself and the way to go back to Him. Though He is in the human form, His real form is that of the Word; and He is in the flesh only to reveal that Word to us and to attach us to it, because only through that Word can we be in touch with the Father.

> He came unto his own, and his own received
> him not.   *(1:11)*

Nobody sent Him to the level of the creation. The Father himself came from His own level by His own sweet will to comfort and release troubled mankind from this vale of tears, but people took Him for just another man like themselves, and rejected Him.

> But as many as received him, to them gave he
> power to become the sons of God, even to them
> that believe in his name.   *(1:12)*

Those who are so fortunate as to understand that the Saints are God himself in the garb of a human being are able to enjoy the Light after getting initiated by a perfect Master, and thus are given the power to see that Light. By "them that believe on his name" is meant those who have faith and follow the teachings. Saint John says: They become the beloved sons of God, or in other words, they themselves become the Lord. Potentially every soul is God, but unless the soul is able to remove those coverings from itself under the guidance of a Master, it can never become God. So there is no question of only one beloved Son of God since the beginning of time.

> Which were born, not of blood, nor of the will of
> the flesh, nor of the will of man, but of God.
> *(1:13)*

John the Baptist was not born like us, by the will of his parents. He did not come to this world because he had karmas. Sins did not pull him to this level. He came by the will of the Father. Mystics who come to this world are not forced, like us, by karmas committed in past births, though they have a mother and a father and come into this world in the same way as other human beings. They come by the order of the Father; they have no karma of their own. They are sent on a mission by God himself, and when it is fulfilled they go back to Him.

> And the Word was made flesh, and dwelt among
> us, . . . full of grace and truth.　　*(1:14)*

Unless God comes in the flesh and dwells amongst us, we can never know Him within ourselves. The Word, or Shabd, is God, and God is the Word, or

Shabd. God, or the Word, came into the flesh, down to our level then—even as He does now in the form of the living Masters—and explained the Way, the Truth, and the Light. In this way He puts us on the path leading back to Him, removes the veil of darkness within us, shows us the true Light, and takes us back to himself. Only then do we recognize and realize God, our Creator.

God is far beyond human comprehension, and unless He comes down to our level to take us back to Him, there is no way out of this mud and mire, this vale of tears, ignorance, and darkness. Every true Master who comes into this world is that Word incarnate, and dwells amongst us.

There is a great difference between the Master and us. He is the Word made flesh, we are just victims of the flesh. The Word, Nam, or Holy Ghost saturates his whole being; but in us it is dormant—smothered and covered by the darkness of our ignorance, our ego. Unless we come across a Master who is the Word made flesh and follow his instructions, we cannot see that Light, we cannot merge back into that Word and become one with the Father.

This contact cannot be made with a Master of the past any more than we can contact God directly, for this is God's method. This is the way He has ordained it and this is why He sends His beloved Sons into the world. He sends them now, He sent them before the time of Christ, He sent them in Christ's time, and He will continue to send them as long as it pleases Him to do so. We must contact a Master, the Word made flesh, while we are in human form, for the human body is the precious gift through which we can make contact with the Supreme Being.

Then Saint John speaks of his successor *(1:15–16)* and goes on to say:

> For the law was given by Moses, but grace and
> truth came by Jesus Christ.   *(1:17)*

This is something very beautiful. It indicates that the teachings are always the same. No true Saint ever brings a new teaching. The same teaching was given by John the Baptist and by Christ as was given in the time of Moses. But the people had lost the true meaning of the teachings of Moses and had become corrupted by commercialism and by priestcraft. They claimed to be following Moses but did not even know what his teachings were. So Christ showed them how to follow the teachings of Moses by revealing to them the grace and truth of the real teachings, which is the purpose of every true Master in his lifetime. It was so in the time of Moses, it was so in the time of Christ, and it is so now.

The real teachings are always the same, but in the course of time they become corrupted by the mind of man; therefore a living Saint is always in the world to bring grace and truth to the genuine seekers. In the time of Christ, it was only through the grace and truth of Jesus Christ that people could really understand the teachings of Moses. And now, those who want to understand the teachings of Christ have to do so through a Master who is living in the world during their lifetime— the Word made flesh in this day and age.

> No man hath seen God at any time; the only
> begotten Son, which is in the bosom of the
> Father, he hath declared him.   *(1:18)*

We cannot see God with our physical eyes, but the Son of the Father, who is also at the level of the Father, sees Him and can enable us to see Him also. Nobody can go back to the Father unless the Father draws him back to himself through His Son. By our own efforts, without His grace, we cannot go back to Him. When the Father wants us to go back to Him, He will put us in touch with His Son, the Word incarnate, the Master who is living at the time that we are in this world.

Here I would like to call your attention to the fact that in many other places in the Bible you will find the expressions, "Sons of God," "the power to become Sons of God," "those who are led by the Spirit are Sons of God," "the manifestation of the Sons of God," "we should be called Sons of God," "now are we the Sons of God." On the other hand, here we have the statement, "the *only* begotten Son of God." This must be a transposition of words and should read, "only the begotten Son of God," for this would coincide with all the other statements in the Bible.

We are all sons of God—but prodigal sons—and can become His true Sons, His begotten Sons, only when we are led by the Spirit, the Holy Ghost, the Shabd, or Word made flesh, back to His bosom.

We know that God sent John the Baptist, and when asked, "Who art thou?" *(1:19–22),* he said:

> I am the voice of one crying in the wilderness,
> Make straight the way of the Lord, as said the
> prophet Esaias.   *(1:23)*

Then the Pharisees *(1:24)* asked him:

> Why baptizest thou then, if thou be not that
> Christ, nor Elias, neither that prophet? *(1:25)*

This question was asked because, according to the
Bible, it was expected that only a Messiah would baptize. John the Baptist evades the question with an indi-
rect answer:

> John answered them, saying, I baptize with
> water: but there standeth one among you,
> whom ye know not;   *(1:26)*

> He it is, who coming after me is preferred be-
> fore me, whose shoe's latchet I am not worthy
> to unloose.   *(1:27)*

Whenever a Mystic comes he baptizes us with
water, meaning the living water, the Nectar, that divine
intoxicant within every one of us at the eye center. The
same water is referred to as the Holy Ghost, the true
Light, the Fire, the Spirit, the Voice of God, the Comforter. It is the Shabd, the Nam—give it any name.
Baptism with physical water is simply symbolic of the
Divine Nectar within. Saints tell us how to withdraw the
soul current back to the eye center so that we may
spiritually drink of this water, or Nectar, hear the Voice
of that Spirit, and see the Light of that Spirit. With the
help of that Voice we know the direction of our Home
within, with the help of that Light we follow the spiritual
path within, and ultimately we go back to our destination, our source of supreme bliss.

John the Baptist knew his end was approaching, that
he would be beheaded, and it was the Father's divine
will that someone should continue to lead people out of
the darkness and show the Light to them. The Father
had sent Jesus to be initiated, or baptized, by John
the Baptist and to appoint him as his successor. John the

Baptist is thus referring to Jesus when he says: There is one among you whom you know not.

Though John the Baptist initiated Jesus and was his Master, he was very humble, as all true Saints are. It was out of humility that he claimed his successor to be greater than he—not that Christ in any way was better than John the Baptist. How could he be better, when in the Gospel according to Saint John, Christ says, "There was a man sent from God, whose name was John."[1] Who can be greater than him who has access to the Father, and who can go back to the Father of his own will?

In reality, all Saints are equal, as all come from the Lord and merge back into Him. But they always want to impress upon their followers the greatness of their successor, for unless they do so, their followers would think that the successor was just one of them and now he is proclaimed a Master. But if the Master himself says, "He is greater than I" or "Greater things he will do," then the seekers and followers will realize that though the successor *was* one of them, he *is* no ordinary human being. If they love their own Master, they will have love and respect for the successor appointed by him. If they do not recognize the successor, they show their lack of faith in their own Master.

If you read their histories, you will find that all Saints, all Mystics, have always talked about the greatness of their successor, but the successors are never ungrateful to their own Master. They always keep their own Master above everyone; for them there is no difference between their Master and God. Only their Master exists for them. Christ acknowledges this when he

---

1. *John 1:6.*

speaks of John the Baptist as a burning and shining light.[1] He says: No woman has ever given birth to a greater soul than to John the Baptist.[2] No greater praise can be given to anybody than that given by Christ to John the Baptist.

Unless a predecessor prepares a way for his successor, nobody will pay any attention to the successor. Even after his Master nominates him publicly, even then people refuse to recognize him, as they are so attached to their own Master. Unless a Master prepares the people for his successor, they will never care for the successor. They will care more for the Master's shoes and Master's bed and Master's table and Master's well and Master's house than for the Master's successor. But because Masters do not want their followers to forget the real teachings and give themselves to these unnecessary rituals and ceremonies, they will always prepare the people for the successor. This is why John the Baptist says: The one who is coming after me is greater than I. He is preparing the people to accept Christ.

> The next day John seeth Jesus coming unto
> him, and saith, Behold the Lamb of God, which
> taketh away the sin of the world.   (1:29)

In those days people used to sacrifice a lamb in atonement for their sins, and John the Baptist wanted to point out to them that Jesus was the real Lamb of God who could take away their sins. Nothing is gained by slaughtering an animal—rather, one adds to one's sins by doing so. But by following the teachings of the real

---

1. *John 5:35.*
2. *Matt. 11:11.*

Lamb of God—the living Master—our sin, or our darkness, is removed and we see the Light. Every Saint uses the background of the people to whom he is speaking in order to help them understand the real teachings. This is why the image of the lamb is used in the Bible.

Then John the Baptist continues praising his successor:

> This is he of whom I said, After me cometh a man which is preferred before me: for he was before me. *(1:30)*

> And I knew him not; but that he should be made manifest to Israel, therefore am I come baptizing with water. *(1:31)*

The word *Israel* means God's chosen people. Spiritually, it does not refer to any particular nationality, but to the true seekers, those whom God has chosen to call back to himself.

> And John bare record, saying, I saw the Spirit descending from heaven like a dove, and it abode upon him. *(1:32)*

> And I knew him not; but he that sent me to baptize with water, the same said unto me, Upon whom thou shalt see the Spirit descending, and remaining on him, the same is he which baptizeth with the Holy Ghost. *(1:33)*

John the Baptist did know Jesus as a person—in fact, was related to him—but he did not reveal the true identity of Jesus until he announced it publicly by stating that it was the Lord who had commissioned him to baptize Jesus. It was God himself who had appointed Jesus as successor to John the Baptist.

As previously indicated, John the Baptist, knowing that his end was approaching, began to prepare his disciples and the seekers of that time by telling them to follow Jesus Christ so that the torch would remain burning.

As a dove descends smoothly and gracefully from a higher place, so did the Shabd, Word, or Holy Ghost come down from the Father and take abode in Jesus. John tells the people that he had himself seen the dove descend upon Christ. This was a spiritual event, internally visible to John, and the only way it could be described to the people was by giving them a physical comparison. Christ was spiritually ready, and all he needed was another Light to light his own candle within. Then not only did his own Light shine, but he also had the power to light the lamps of the genuine seekers living in his time.

So John the Baptist declared himself a witness to the fact that Christ was fit to put seekers on the spiritual path and take them back to the Father. Potentially, Jesus was a Master from the time of his birth. Such souls are prepared, even at the time of their birth, to become a Master when they come in contact with their Master. They are ready, and it takes only the contact with a living Master for them to be able to function in that capacity. Every soul who has become a Master is practically ready, but still he needs the "spark" of a living Master to give him Light. Jesus actually became a Master, or Christ, when he was baptized, or initiated, at which time his spirit ascended to the Father and descended, and he was appointed successor by John the Baptist, as commanded by the Father.

And I saw, and bare record that this is the Son of
God.   *(1:34)*

In the next few chapters we find that two of John's
disciples heard him speak, and they followed Jesus.
When Jesus inquired of them what they wanted, they
asked him where he dwelled. So he invited them to
come and see. "They came and saw where he dwelt, and
abode with him that day: for it was about the tenth
hour" *(1:39)*. One of the two who followed Jesus after
hearing John speak was Andrew, Simon Peter's brother.
He first finds his own brother, Simon (Peter), and ex-
claims, "We have found the Messias" *(1:41)*, which
means they recognized not one, but two perfect living
Masters: John the Baptist and his successor, Jesus
Christ.

It is very interesting to note that in that particular
verse Saint John has used the word *Messias,* which
implies more than one *Messia (Messiah)*. If this word is
researched from the original writings, it will be seen
that it means more than one. However, even in the
Gospel according to Saint John, in order to end up with
one Christ, or Messiah, one Son of God, this phrase is
inserted in the verse *(1:41):* "which is, being interpreted, the Christ." If you read it without that phrase,
the interpreters would have to admit that there were two
Christs, Messiahs, or living Masters—John the Baptist
and Jesus Christ—at that time.

Then Andrew brought Simon (Peter) to Jesus. "And
when Jesus beheld him, he said, Thou art Simon the son
of Jona" *(1:42)*, and that is when he named him Cephas
or Peter, which means a rock, or a stone. Then Jesus
went forth into Galilee and found Philip and said unto
him, "Follow me" *(1:43)*. Philip found Nathanael and

said to him, "We have found him, of whom Moses in the law, and the prophets, did write, Jesus of Nazareth, the son of Joseph" *(1:45)*. When Nathanael inquired if anything good could come out of Nazareth, Philip invited him to come and see for himself. When Jesus saw Nathanael coming to him, he said, "Behold an Israelite indeed, in whom is no guile!" *(1:47)*. Nathanael was surprised that Jesus knew him and exclaimed, "Rabbi, thou art the Son of God; thou are the King of Israel" *(1:49)*. And Jesus replied, "Because I said unto thee, I saw thee under the fig tree, believest thou? thou shalt see greater things than these" *(1:50)*.

Later, Jesus said to Nathanael:

> Verily, verily, I say unto you, Hereafter ye shall see heaven open and the angels of God ascending and descending upon the Son of man. *(1:51)*

Since the Shabd, the Holy Ghost, has taken abode in Christ, the gates of heaven are open to him. Now, by means of that very Sound Current, the Shabd, Christ can go back to the Father and come back to this earth, just as he wishes. He can be in the flesh and also in the bosom of the Father. By means of the Sound Current he can ascend to heaven and descend back to the body whenever he wishes to do so. And he tells Nathanael, "hereafter"—meaning, after Nathanael is initiated, he will see heaven open and will know the full glory of Christ, his Master.

2

Jesus, his mother, and his disciples were among the guests at a wedding feast. When the supply of wine[1] was exhausted the mother of Jesus informed him of this, indicating that he should perform a miracle. Jesus answered:

> . . . mine hour is not yet come.   *(2:4)*

The Masters come into this world at a particular time and for a particular purpose. They perform their allotted task at a time and place that is designated by the Father.

Masters do not come to perform miracles in this world. Miracles do happen in their lifetime, but that is not their purpose in coming to the world. The real miracle that a Saint can and does perform is his giving us spiritual initiation—a new birth, which puts us in touch with the Word, the Holy Ghost—without which we can never be saved from the cycles of birth and death, nor ever see the kingdom of God within us.

The mother of Jesus told the servants to do whatever Jesus asked of them, so they filled large pots with water as directed by Jesus, and it is said that he changed the water into wine.

---

1. The "wine" in this instance does not necessarily mean the alcoholic beverage, as this word is used for describing the fermented as well as the unfermented juice of any fruit.

After this he went down to Capernaum, he, and
his mother, and his brethren, and his disciples:
and they continued there not many days. *(2:12)*

And the Jews' passover was at hand, and Jesus
went up to Jerusalem,   *(2:13)*

And found in the temple those that sold oxen
and sheep and doves, and the changers of money
sitting: *(2:14)*

And when he had made a scourge of small
cords, he drove them all out of the temple, and
the sheep, and the oxen; and poured out the
changers' money, and overthrew the tables;
                                         (2:15)

And said unto them that sold doves, Take these
things hence; make not my Father's house an
house of merchandise.   *(2:16)*

When Christ went to the temple, he found that the
teachings of John the Baptist and Moses were being
exploited by self-interested people. Generally after the
death of a Mystic, selfish people try to exploit others in
the name of the Mystic and try to sell his teachings. So
Christ told the people who were managing the temple:
Never commercialize any Mystic's teachings. Do not
try to fill your pockets. Naturally they started murmuring because this practice was bread and butter for them.
Then Christ tells them:

Destroy this temple, and in three days I will
raise it up.   *(2:19)*

He says: However beautiful or imposing a temple
may be, you can always build it again if it is destroyed.

After all, it is only made of stone and mortar. You can always build it again in no time—"in three days" means in no time—but if you destroy this body, the temple of the living God,[1] where the Lord himself lives, you cannot rebuild it. Once you lose this human form, you will not get it again so easily. The Lord does not stay in these temples of brick and mortar that we make for His residence. He is right within your body; but, says Christ, you do not bother to seek Him in your body. You worship the Father in these manmade temples. You do not care for the temple that the Lord has given you and in which He resides. He calls the human body the temple of the living God, because in this temple and in no other can we live with God and become God.

The Lord has given us this human form just for one purpose: to realize Him. If we misuse or destroy this temple by remaining attached to worldly treasures, we will not get this opportunity of the human form again so easily.

---

1. "Know ye not that ye are the temple of God, and that the Spirit of God dwelleth in you? *(1 Cor. 3:16).*
   ". . . for ye are the temple of the living God" *(2 Cor. 6:16).*

3

While Jesus was in Jerusalem, a high-ranking member of the Pharisees named Nicodemus, who was himself "a ruler of the Jews" and "a master of Israel," came to Jesus to inquire about his teachings. He recognized that Jesus was from God and wanted to hear what Jesus had to say. But Nicodemus, though not hostile to Jesus as most of the Pharisees were, did not want to make a public show of going to Jesus, so he came to Jesus "by night" and asked him questions.

> Jesus answered and said unto him, Verily, verily, I say unto thee, Except a man be born again, he cannot see the kingdom of God. (3:3)

> Nicodemus saith unto him, How can a man be born when he is old? can he enter the second time into his mother's womb, and be born? (3:4)

> Jesus answered, Verily, verily I say unto thee, Except a man be born of water and of the Spirit, he cannot enter into the kingdom of God. (3:5)

> That which is born of the flesh is flesh; and that which is born of the Spirit is spirit. (3:6)

> Marvel not that I said unto thee, Ye must be born again. (3:7)

Here Jesus explains to Nicodemus that he must be "born again" if he wants to see the kingdom of God.

Naturally, to one who has had no spiritual experience, to be born again seems impossible. Nicodemus, though a "master" of Israel, is a man of formal religion and reacts as any worldly person would when he asks, How can this be? One cannot return to the womb and be reborn. Jesus says to Nicodemus that he is confusing physical rebirth with the spiritual rebirth that Jesus is talking about. Jesus then expresses the same concept in simpler language when he says, "That which is born of the flesh is flesh: and that which is born of the Spirit is spirit." He points out that to be born of the Spirit is the new birth he speaks of; and that being born of water means being born of living water, the Nectar within; so being born of the Spirit means being born of the Sound, the Word, the Holy Ghost. So the whole discussion refers to the spiritual initiation, when one is put on the path leading back to God. That, in a nutshell, is being born again.

After being born in this world we begin to grow and develop physically; and after receiving initiation, or baptism, the spiritual birth, we grow and develop spiritually.

What Jesus tells Nicodemus is consistent with what all Mystics teach: that within every one of us there is Sound and Light, which can be experienced within at the eye center. As pointed out earlier, the soul and the mind have their seat, or headquarters, at the center between the two eyes, the place where all our attention is to be concentrated in order to see that Light and hear that Sound within.

When we compare the two phrases, "Except a man be born again, he cannot see the kingdom of God" and "Except a man be born of water and of the Spirit, he

cannot enter into the kingdom of God,"[1] with the statement of John the Baptist when he answered the priests
and Levites, "I baptize with water,"[2] he was doing
exactly what Jesus later said was essential for entering
God's kingdom.

The soul has two faculties: that of seeing and that of
hearing within. The Lord has kept the Sound and Light
within every one of us, but as mentioned earlier, we
cannot see this Light and hear this Sound within the
temple of our body because of the veil of darkness
between us and the Father. If we are attached to the
flesh, we always take birth into the flesh again. But if we
are attached to the Spirit within, then we take birth into
the Spirit. When we are attached to the senses, we come
back into the flesh; but attaching ourselves to the Spirit
gives us birth in heaven. When we become the Spirit,
the Word, only then do we get peace. That is taking a
new spiritual birth.

When a Mystic initiates us into a new birth, he gives
us the technique of withdrawing our soul current to the
eye center, where we can hear the Spirit, or Sound, and
see that Light. It is by means of the Sound and the Light
that we travel on the spiritual path back to the Father's
house. So the day of our initiation into the spiritual path
is the beginning of the process of spiritual growth.

Then Jesus makes it still clearer:

> The wind bloweth where it listeth, and thou
> hearest the sound thereof, but canst not tell
> whence it cometh, and whither it goeth: so is
> every one that is born of the Spirit.   (3:8)

---

1. *John 3:3, 5.*
2. *John 1:26.*

He says: What do I mean by taking birth into the Spirit? Taking birth into the Spirit means that when you are able to withdraw your consciousness to the eye center and still your mind there, you hear a Sound within yourself, and in the beginning that Sound resembles the blowing of the wind. You will not be able to know from which direction it is coming—whether it is coming from the right, whether it is coming from the left, whether it is coming from above, whether it is coming from beneath. When you are hearing that Sound and seeing that Light, then you have taken birth into the Spirit. That is taking a new spiritual birth.

To be born of the Spirit, says Jesus, is to be in touch with the Word, the Sound Current, which is within every one of us. But we cannot contact the Sound unless we are able to withdraw our consciousness to the eye center and hold our mind motionless there. In the beginning the Sound—that is, the sound of the Spirit—resembles the blowing or rushing of the wind. Though we hear it, we do not know from which direction it is coming, whether from above or below, from the left or the right. When we attach ourself to the Sound, it takes us to its source, the Lord himself. To take a new birth is to be in touch with that Shabd, or Word. This is what is meant by "so is every one that is born of the Spirit."

> Nicodemus answered and said unto him, How can these things be?   (3:9)

> Jesus answered and said unto him, Art thou a master of Israel, and knowest not these things?
> (3:10)

Nicodemus is still astonished and asks, How can this be? Although he is a "master" of Israel, he is only performing rituals and ceremonies. He has not had any spiritual experience within himself. The mystic truths had been lost to the people of that time, even though Moses and some of the biblical prophets had been Mystics and had taught the same truths. But not until the time of John the Baptist and Jesus had anyone come to revive the same original and timeless Truth which the Hebrews had received from Moses, but had lost over the years.

Nicodemus held the office of master and was viewed by the people of Israel as a spiritually enlightened person, to be looked to for their spiritual needs. But the real spiritual path to God had long been lost to the priests and the people. So when Jesus explained the true spiritual path to Nicodemus, at first Nicodemus was skeptical, but he did receive the teachings later.

Here was a master of Israel who had no personal spiritual experience, because that knowledge had been lost to him as he had no perfect Master. And Jesus came to revive the teachings that had been lost.

> Verily, verily, I say unto thee, We speak that we do know, and testify that we have seen: and ye receive not our witness.   *(3:11)*
>
> If I have told you earthly things, and ye believe not, how shall ye believe, if I tell you of heavenly things?   *(3:12)*

As in the case with all true Masters, Jesus then proceeds to assure Nicodemus that what Jesus speaks of is not hearsay, but what he himself has seen and experienced within. The Masters teach only that which they know from experience—not mere book knowledge, although they do quote scriptures to help us

understand the spiritual path from our own background
and to prove that the teachings of all the Saints are the
same. They emphasize the need of a living Master,
without whom we cannot begin to follow their teachings. Christ then says: In spite of my speaking to you
from my personal experience, you do not believe what I
say. So Jesus cautions Nicodemus: If you have so many
doubts and do not believe what I tell you about earthly
things, then how will you believe what I tell you about
my Father and other spiritual matters?

Once we are fortunate enough to be initiated by a
Master and put on the path, we should have absolute
faith in him. Only he knows what is best for us, because
he can see the past, present, and future at a glance. We
are confused even by the problems of this world; how
can we know what is good for our spiritual progress?

Christ then continues to present further evidence to
Nicodemus:

> And no man hath ascended up to heaven, but he
> that came down from heaven, even the Son of
> man which is in heaven.   *(3:13)*

Jesus says that no man can go back to the Father
unless he contacts a Master who has come from the
Father. Even Christ, the Son of man, could not go back
to the Father until he had been initiated, or baptized, by
John the Baptist, who came from the Father. As mentioned earlier, "There was a man sent from God, whose
name was John." Even a Master needs a Master before
he actually becomes a Master.

Everyone who wants to go back to the Father needs
a living Master, for if we could go back by our own
efforts there would never have been a need for Christ or

any other redeemers to come into this world. So unless we seek initiation from a Master who has been sent by the Father, we cannot go back to the Father. This is a divine law, taught by every true Master.

> And as Moses lifted up the serpent in the wilderness, even so must the Son of man be lifted up:
> *(3:14)*

> That whosoever believeth in him should not perish, but have eternal life. *(3:15)*

Christ is saying here that our consciousness must be lifted up or awakened so that we are no longer controlled by the senses, but by the Spirit. As long as we are slaves of the mind and senses—also portrayed in the Bible as a serpent—we are anchored in the mire of this world; but as soon as we are attached to the Shabd, the Word, our heavy chains and bonds are loosened. Then our attention can make its home in the eye center and be lifted up, until we finally merge into the Word, which will take us to the Father. Then we will not perish; we will not have to face birth and death again, but will have eternal life—in the bosom of the heavenly Father.

Another directive given by Christ is that if you come across a man who has come from the Father and who has access to the Father, believe in him. The word *believe* has a very deep meaning. What is *believing* in a Saint? We have to believe and have faith that he has come from the Father to our level; that being at our level he is also at the level of the Father; that he is the one who can guide us back to the Father; that we have to follow all his instructions and mold our life according to his teachings. That is believing in the Master.

Believing and having faith in a Mystic means to follow his teachings and to take a new birth, by God's grace. Christ says: Then you will not perish. Now we are perishing—we leave this body, and another body is ready for us; we face death, and another round of birth and death is ready for us to face. Now we are moving from "house" to "house"—from body to body. But when we believe and have faith in a Mystic and live his teachings, we are given a new birth, a spiritual birth, through his initiation, and go to that place where we need not face birth and death again, where we will have eternal life.

> For God so loved the world, that he gave his
> only begotten Son, that whosoever believeth in
> him should not perish, but have everlasting life.
> *(3:16)*

Jesus points out that the Lord has given to His beloved Sons the privilege of taking us back to Him. No one else has this privilege. Who are the beloved Sons?[1] They are those who have experienced the Light within themselves through initiation by a Master, have gone back to the level of the Father while in the human body, and have been directed by Him, through their own Master, to take back to the Father the souls allotted to them. They thus become His beloved Sons, through whom the Father can be reached.

People are often baffled when they read that He gave His only begotten Son. As was explained earlier *(1:18)*, this must be a transposition of words and should read, "only His begotten Son." If the word "only" comes

---

1. This was also explained earlier in 1:18.

before "His," it then coincides with all the other biblical references to "Sons of God," and also conforms to the teachings of all other Mystics in the world.

There is no question of only one Son of the Father. John the Baptist was also His Son; as Saint John says, "There was a man sent from God, whose name was John." Having come from God to our level, he had access to the Father and was His Son. Moses and so many other Mystics were also Sons of the Father, but they could lead us only while they were alive, while they were in the flesh. They could lead only those people whom they contacted while in the human body, only those who believed in them, who lived their teachings, and who had a new birth (initiation) through them. Only those people could obtain spiritual guidance from the Mystics; they also could become the children of Light, the sons of the Father, and merge back into the Father.

As mentioned in the beginning, it is a pity that Christ himself did not write the Bible. Neither was it written by him nor were any notes taken when he was giving his sermons. His teachings were written long after he was crucified and were translated from one language to another many times, so naturally much has been lost. We therefore cannot interpret the Bible word for word, as a book of law.

> For God sent not his Son into the world to condemn the world; but that the world through him might be saved.   *(3:17)*

> He that believeth on him is not condemned: but he that believeth not is condemned already, because he hath not believed in the name of the only begotten Son of God.   *(3:18)*

> And this is the condemnation, that light is come
> into the world, and men loved darkness rather
> than light, because their deeds were evil. *(3:19)*

> For every one that doeth evil hateth the light,
> neither cometh to the light, lest his deeds
> should be reproved.   *(3:20)*

> But he that doeth the truth cometh to the light,
> that his deeds may be made manifest, that they
> are wrought in God.   *(3:21)*

Here Jesus tells us that Saints do not come into the world to judge our weaknesses or to condemn us for our sins. They come with mercy and grace, to help and guide us back to the Father. We should have faith and confidence in them.

We are already condemned in this world. What greater condemnation can there be than being separated from the Father and living in misery! Saints come only to redeem us. They come to take us out of this world, back to the Father. They come to save their disciples from the cycle of birth and death, from the cycle of transmigration of the soul. "That the world through *him* might be saved" means through the living Master of the time, as Christ was in his time.

Christ indicates that whoever believes in a Mystic will never be condemned. He will be saved from birth and death. Believing in a Mystic means following his teachings, living his teachings, receiving baptism, or initiation, from him, and with his help withdrawing to the eye center and attaching oneself to that Spirit within.

The living Light in the garb of a perfect Master is here in the world. The living Light can lead people from the darkness back to the Creator, and yet they do not believe in that living Light, in that Word made flesh. It is a pity that they are happy to live in the attachments of the world.

The Saints come to our level; they can help us to eliminate the darkness; they can take us back to the Father, but we have no faith in them and do not *practice* what they teach. Light is there, but we do not want to follow that Light. So we remain away from the Father. This is our condemnation.

Those who love evil and bad deeds, and are victims of the senses, always want to live in darkness, always want to remain immersed in sensual pleasures. But those who do good deeds want to live in the Light. And those "that doeth the truth" are those who are initiated and traveling on the path of Light and Sound, on their way back to God.

> Then there arose a question between some of
> John's disciples and the Jews about purifying.
> (3:25)

> And they came unto John, and said unto him,
> Rabbi, he that was with thee beyond Jordan, to
> whom thou barest witness, behold, the same
> baptizeth, and all men come to him. (3:26)

After Jesus had explained his teachings to Nicodemus, he went to Judea where he baptized, or initiated, those who came to him. At the same time John the Baptist was also baptizing in another place, for he was not yet imprisoned. Thus, according to the Gospel, two Masters were baptizing at the same time and at places not far apart. Some of John's disciples came to John with a question about purifying, or washing away of karmas, and also informed him that Jesus was baptizing, or initiating, people just as their Master, John, was doing, and that people were going to Jesus for initiation. This puzzled John's disciples, so he put them at ease with his answer.

> John answered and said, A man can receive
> nothing, except it be given him from heaven.
>   *(3:27)*

John the Baptist's answer points out a fundamentally important law of the Creator: that each Master has been allotted a certain number of "sheep" to initiate and take home to the Father, and that only the Father determines which souls are for which Mystic.

John explains to his disciples that Jesus can initiate only those souls which have been marked for Jesus and given to him by the Father, just as John's disciples had been marked and given to John by the Father. John points out that when he baptized Jesus he recognized him as a Son of God, a Master, and that it was no surprise that they were each initiating, or baptizing, at the same time, as they were both doing the Father's work.

Further, John's answer makes it clear that whatever we receive, we receive as a result of the Father's will. No one can approach God in heaven unless He wants to be approached. "A man can receive nothing except it be given from heaven."

The seeker is moved through the Father's love—when it is showered on him—to search for a living Master. The Father creates an urge in those marked by Him to merge back into Him; and unless that urge is within them, they will never even think about the

Father. God attracts us by His love, through the Master. When we are accepted by a Master, we find that we are on the path leading to the Father.

Gold becomes pure when it passes through fire. Similarly, the love that the Lord gives us burns and consumes all our impurities and makes us pure gold. But first He gives us His love. None else can give us that love, nor is it in our hands to get that love. We do not get it by our own effort or with our intellect. Only by His grace do we get it, and then these impurities are automatically burned or consumed. No matter how much credit we may claim, it is all His gift, and He has His own ways and means to give us that fire of love.

John the Baptist then gives his disciples even more assurance when he tells them:

> Ye yourselves bear me witness, that I said, I am
> not the Christ, but that I am sent before him.
> *(3:28)*

It is also important to notice that when John denied that he was the Christ, he was being consistent with the Jewish tradition. A Master generally does not make public claim to being a Master. John does not do so here, nor does there seem to be any biblical evidence that Jesus ever called himself "Christ."

Then, in the form of a parable, John the Baptist further reassures his disciples:

> He that hath the bride is the bridegroom: but the
> friend of the bridegroom, which standeth and
> heareth him, rejoiceth greatly because of the
> bridegroom's voice: this my joy therefore is
> fulfilled. *(3:29)*

This is truly a beautiful parable. A bridegroom is happy because he is marrying a beautiful girl. But why do his relatives and friends also become happy? They are not getting the bride. They are happy because their friend, the bridegroom, is happy, and they rejoice in his happiness.

Through this parable John points out that Jesus is the bridegroom and the Lord is the bride. Jesus has become one with the Lord through the initiation that John has performed, and John knows that Jesus, by initiating the souls that have been marked for him. is carrying out the will of the Lord, which makes John happy. John's happiness is like the happiness of the bridegroom's friend in the parable, and is the result of the happiness that Jesus has in doing the will of the Lord.

Saints are one with the Father, and this oneness gives them spiritual bliss. When we go in their company we share in their happiness, even though we have not yet enjoyed those inner spiritual realms nor seen the Father.

If we go to a happy person, he will make us happy in no time. As the Saints are one with God, they cannot help radiating happiness, and when we are in their presence we also share their contentment, bliss, and peace, though our inner eye has not yet been opened.

Even before we are able to travel on the inner path, the very association with or company of a Mystic makes us feel relaxed and happy. A man with eyes enjoys both the beauty and the fragrance of a flower, but even a blind man can enjoy the fragrance of the flower. Before we make progress on the spiritual path we are all spiritually blind, but even then we can enjoy the spiritual fragrance of the Master. When our inner eye is opened through the technique given to us by the Master at the time of initiation, we too can enjoy the beauty of those spiritual experiences within.

> He must increase, but I must decrease. *(3:30)*

John the Baptist knows that he is not long for this world and his work is coming to an end. He also knows which souls are marked for him and realizes that his work is approaching its end, as is his life in this world. At the same time, he recognizes that Jesus is just beginning to initiate the souls that are marked for Jesus. Therefore John points out that the work of Jesus must increase, but his own work must decrease.

> He that cometh from above is above all: he that
> is of the earth is earthly, and speaketh of the
> earth: he that cometh from heaven is above all.
> *(3:31)*

One who has come from the Father is above all, which means he is not attached to anything of this creation. He is attached only to the Creator. Though the Father is within every one of us, we are separated from Him by a veil of darkness and we do not see Him. Having come to the earth, we are attached to this creation, but the Mystics are attached to the Creator. What John speaks of here is similar to what Jesus later says.[1]

Because the Master comes from heaven, he always talks of heaven and peace, he always creates the longing and desire in us to go back to our Father—our source and destination. He also makes us happy because he

---

1. "Ye are from beneath; I am from above: ye are of this world; I am not of this world" *(John 8:23)*.

puts us on the path that he has himself followed. People of the world are interested only in talking of worldly things. But once we are happily started on the path these things do not interest us, because they are trivial compared with the happiness which we taste and which is eternal.

Then John the Baptist says:

> And what he hath seen and heard, that he testifieth; and no man receiveth his testimony.
> (3:32)

> He that hath received his testimony hath set to his seal that God is true.   (3:33)

This is similar to what Jesus said earlier to Nicodemus (3:11), that a perfect living Master speaks from experience, not from hearsay. He declares those spiritual truths which he has seen and heard from the Father within. But though he speaks from personal knowledge and experience, people have difficulty believing him.

John then goes on to say that they who have been accepted by a Master and have themselves had spiritual experience within are willing to testify that God is true and can be experienced within.

John the Baptist continues:

> For he whom God hath sent speaketh the words of God: for God giveth not the spirit by measure unto him.   (3:34)

> The Father loveth the Son, and hath given all things into his hand.   (3:35)

This shows the infinite mercy and grace of God through His Sons—the Saints, or Masters. They are extremely generous; they disregard their own comforts and even physical needs in order to teach us the words of God. And the Spirit, or the Word, the Shabd, is not meted out or rationed out to us in small portions. The supply is infinite, and all we need to do is to empty ourselves of our worldly desires, our ego, and the Father will fill us with all things—that is, His all-embracing love—through His Son, our Master. The Saints try to create in us the longing to return to the Father. They never tire of talking about God and the way to realize Him within ourselves. They always radiate and share their happiness with us.

> He that believeth on the Son hath everlasting life: and he that believeth not the Son shall not see life; but the wrath of God abideth on him.
> *(3:36)*

This means that one who has faith in the Son, the Master, and follows his teachings, will have everlasting life—not that he will stay in the world forever; who wants to stay in this world of pleasure and pain, of ever-changing circumstances? Nothing is everlasting or permanent here. When we have faith in the Son and follow the path, we will have no attachments to bring us back to this world; so when we die we will have everlasting life in the spiritual realm of the Father. But one who does not believe in the Son will not follow the path, so he will not see or enjoy that eternal, everlasting life. Therefore "the wrath of God abideth on him," because he remains separated from God, and remains confused and frustrated.

4

Jesus therefore, being wearied with his journey,
sat thus on the well: and it was about the sixth
hour.   *(4:6)*

There cometh a woman of Samaria to draw
water: Jesus saith unto her, Give me to drink.
                                               (4:7)

Then this Samaritan woman, being a member of a
sect normally despised by the orthodox Jews, asked
Jesus:

How is it that thou, being a Jew, askest drink of
me, which am a woman of Samaria?   *(4:9)*

Jesus answered and said unto her, If thou
knewest the gift of God, and who it is that saith
to thee, Give me to drink; thou wouldest have
asked of him, and he would have given thee
living water.   *(4:10)*

Christ's answer shows clearly that even if the Sa-
maritans are not recognized by the Jews nor by the
Gentiles, as far as the soul is concerned there is no
difference between high and low class or caste, color or
nationality. Whoever sincerely longs to meet God can
get this living water, which will take him back to the
Lord and thus give him eternal life. The living water is
not to be confused with the water of this world, for it

refers to the Divine Nectar within every one of us. It is only through a living Master, such as Christ was in his time, that one can get this living water, also called the Word, Shabd, Nam, Amrit ('Nectar of Immortality'), the Sound Current, and many other names. So Jesus says to her: Do not worry about your being a Samaritan—that is not important. The important thing is the Shabd, the living water. Similarly, when we meet a Master we should ask of him only one thing, and that is the living water, the Shabd. Then he says:

> Whosoever drinketh of this water shall thirst
> again.   *(4:13)*

The Lord may give us *anything* of this world. Howsoever rich we may be—we may have billions of dollars in our bank balance—we are always thirsty for more. We are never contented. We are never happy. We always want more, more, and even more. The more we have, the more we need, the more we want. A king wants more kingdoms, a rich person wants more riches. Whatever honor the Lord may give us in this creation does not make us happy. We are still hankering for more power, more honor. There is no contentment within us.

All the pleasures that we try to get outside are short-lived. They do not give us peace forever, because at the base of every pleasure is a fear of losing that pleasure. As long as that fear is there, one can never be happy. If you get wealth, there is a fear of losing it: the bank may fail, your friends may cheat you, or dacoits may loot you. That fear is always there. You are happy to be married, but then the fear is there that your wife may desert you, she may be unfaithful to you, she may become sick, she may die.

But whosoever drinketh of the water that I shall
give him shall never thirst; but the water that I
shall give him shall be in him a well of water
springing up into everlasting life.   *(4:14)*

Christ says: If you follow my teachings and taste the
water that I will give you, meaning the "water" that I can
help you to obtain from within yourself, then you will
never be thirsty. Then you will have no desires of the
world. You will have only one desire: to merge back into
the Father. Then you will be the most contented person,
the king of kings.

"But the water that I shall give him shall be in him
a well of water springing up into everlasting life." He
says: I am not going to give you anything from myself. The Lord has already kept that water—that Spirit,
that Nectar, that living water—within every one of us,
and that water is "springing up into everlasting life."
"Springing" means it never dies. Christ says: At the eye
center, that living water is spouting like a fountain that
never dries, but our cup is upside down.

If a cup is upside down, not a drop of water can come
into it, howsoever it may rain. The moment we put the
cup in the right position, the cup is filled with rainwater.
Similarly, Christ says, that living water is at the eye
center within every one of us, but our cup is inverted.
The soul has taken the association of the mind, and the
tendency of the mind is downward towards the senses.
The living water is at the eye center, flowing like a
spring, but it is of no use to us unless we put our cup in
the right position.

When a Mystic puts us on the path, he gives us the
technique of withdrawing our consciousness up to the
eye center so that the cup is right side up. Then our cup

is filled with that living water springing within every one of us "unto everlasting life." Once we taste that Nectar within ourself, we will have everlasting life. Our desires, our karmas, our attachments, are pulling us back to this creation. When we are no longer attached to the world, when we are able to wash away all the sins we have committed in past births, then nobody can pull us back to this creation. And that we can achieve only if we drink the Nectar within ourself.

Unless the mind gets something better than the worldly pleasures, it is never content. The living water is so sweet, so full of joy and bliss, that once we taste it we experience much greater joy than anything we could ever dream of getting in this world. We merge into the Giver, the Creator himself. When we have the Giver, we no longer want the gifts of the world; we are in touch with the Creator rather than with His creation.

Then the woman told Christ:

> Our fathers worshipped in this mountain; and
> ye say, that in Jerusalem is the place where men
> ought to worship.   (4:20)

She says: Our fathers have always believed that by going to the mountain where Moses realized the Father within himself, perhaps they also could realize the Father. But because Christ had come from Jerusalem, she thought he was telling people they should go to Jerusalem to worship the Father. So Christ explains to her:

> Woman, believe me, the hour cometh, when ye
> shall neither in this mountain, nor yet at Jerusa-
> lem, worship the Father.   (4:21)

He knew that this soul would be initiated. He says: You were being misled in trying to find the Father in the mountains or in Jerusalem. The Father is not hiding himself in Jerusalem; the Father is not hiding himself in a mountain. He lives within you, and your time has come now when you will know how to worship the Father, because you have come to me. You are going to follow me and I am going to baptize you.

> Ye worship ye know not what: we know what we
> worship.   *(4:22)*

He says: People think they worship the Father but they do not know the Father. Unless they know the Father, how can they worship Him? How can they love Him? They have their own mental concept of the Father and they are happy only in that. But the time has come when you will know how to worship the Father. And what is that worship?

> But the hour cometh, and now is, when the true
> worshippers shall worship the Father in spirit
> and in truth: for the Father seeketh such to
> worship him.   *(4:23)*

He says: The true worshipper always worships the Father in Spirit. Unless you worship the Father in Spirit, you are not worshipping the Father at all. You are only living in your own mental concept of the Father, and this concept will not lead you anywhere except to the darkness of illusion.

"For the Father seeketh such to worship him." He says: Your Father wants to be worshipped in Spirit. If you do not worship the Father in Spirit, then you are not worshipping Him; you are worshipping something that actually does not exist. You are worshipping your own mental image of the Father. He says to the woman: But do not worry, you have come to me and I will now tell you how to worship the Father in Spirit.

> God is a Spirit: and they that worship him must
> worship him in spirit and in truth.   *(4:24)*

Why should we worship the Spirit? Jesus says: Because God is Spirit. There is no difference between the Spirit, or the Word, and the Father. In the beginning he had explained to us that the Word, the Creative Power, and the Father are one and the same. If we are in touch with the Word within, we are in touch with God. So he says: Worship of the Spirit is worship of God.

There is no ritual or ceremony in worshipping the Father. You do not have to go through any austerities to find Him. As long as your attention is below the eye center, and you are trying to seek the Father outside in a temple or a synagogue, in a book, in some holy tank, in the mountains, or in Jerusalem, you are not worshipping the Father at all. When you are able to withdraw your consciousness to the eye center and are one with the Voice of God within, then you are worshipping the Father. The Father has His own divine law of how to worship Him: we must worship Him in Spirit and in Truth.

As you know, his disciples asked Jesus to eat some food.

> But he said unto them, I have meat to eat that ye
> know not of.   *(4:32)*

Why do we eat food? Just to sustain the body. But by eating food, we do not sustain our soul. The real purpose for which we were created is to worship the Father and merge back into Him, and we cannot achieve that purpose unless we are on the path. So Jesus indicates that he has something much higher than the food of this world on which to live. My "meat" is the Word—the Shabd, or Nam—he says. That sustains me and gives me life.

> My meat is to do the will of him that sent me,
> and to finish his work.   (4:34)

I have been sent into this world by the Father with a definite purpose in view, and that purpose is to finish His work. My work is to live in the will of Him who sent me. I have not come to your level by my will or by the will of my parents or by the will of karma. I have come by the will of my Father, to do His work, and I want to live in His will because I have no will of my own—I have risen above the realm of mind and illusion. Now you are living according to the will of your mind, and that is not "living" at all.

> Say not ye, There are yet four months, and then
> cometh harvest?   (4:35)

He says: We always make excuses—"Why worship the Father so soon? We are still young and have small children; when we grow older we will have enough money to our credit. Then we will retire from our work and find some lonely corner or some lonely beach where we can worship the Father." We always like to give the worst part of our life for worshipping the Father.

When we are young, we give ourselves to the sensual pleasures; we give ourselves to worldly work. And when we become old, when we cannot enjoy the senses anymore, when the senses refuse to cooperate with us, we think about the Father. We want to devote only that part of life to the Father. How much can we worship the Father then? We must give the best part of our life to the Father, not the worst part. It is a very rare opportunity to be in the human form. And it is only while we are in the human form that we can worship the Lord and go back to Him. So Christ is impressing upon us not to put off the worship with one excuse or another.

"There are yet four months" means: You say, there is plenty of time to apply ourselves to spiritual work— we are young, let us enjoy the pleasures of the world, and when we are older there will be enough time for meditation. The truth is, if you come onto the path at a young age, at least you do not collect much rubbish, much load. You cannot say that an elderly person can devote more time to meditation. His mind is more scattered. He has spread too many deep roots in this world and he has to pull out every root. If a young man does not allow the roots to spread, it becomes easier for him to pull them out. Whosoever gets the opportunity to be on the path—whenever he gets initiated—should try to do his best.

> . . . behold, I say unto you, Lift up your eyes,
> and look on the fields; for they are white already
> to harvest.   (4:35)

To "lift up your eyes" means to lift up your consciousness to the level of the eye center. In our body, the seat of the soul and mind knotted together is at the eye center. If we want to recollect something we have forgotten, our hand automatically moves to the forehead. We never place our hands on any other part of the body to recollect what we have forgotten. So this place has something to do with our thinking center. This is also referred to by Christ as the single eye or the door of our house.[1] From the eye center our soul is being pulled down by the senses, and our consciousness is spread into the whole world through the nine apertures of the body (the two eyes, the two ears, the two nostrils, the mouth, and the two lower apertures). So Christ says: As long as you are living below the eye center, you are not worshipping the Father; you are not in touch with the Spirit. If you want to make the best use of the human form, "lift up your eyes." Lift up your consciousness to the eye center.

Withdrawing our consciousness up to the eye center, where the mind can be stilled, is also referred to in Psalms: "Be still, and know that I am God."[2] Our spiritual journey starts from the eye center, and only after we have stilled the mind at this point, according to the instructions of our Master, can we know God.

Christ says: When you are able to *be* at the eye center and still your mind there, then "look to the fields; for they are white already to harvest." When you have raised your consciousness to the eye center, you have, as it were, the crop of your meditation ripe and ready for harvesting, and you can begin to gather it. He says: The Lord is always waiting for you there. The Nectar is flowing there day and night. The ringing radiance, that

---

1. *Matt. 6:22, 7:7.*
2. *Psalms 46:10.*

Spirit, is there day and night, waiting to pull you to your own destination, your eternal home of peace and bliss.

But not until you lift up your consciousness to the eye center, can you be in touch with that Spirit, the Father, and go back to your destination, your source. So he says: Do not put off your meditation on one excuse or another. Make the best use of your time and withdraw your soul current to the eye center. The harvest is ready for you; the Lord is waiting for you there.

> And he that reapeth receiveth wages, and gathereth fruit unto life eternal: that both he that soweth and he that reapeth may rejoice together.   *(4:36)*

This is very beautiful. Whosoever works hard is well rewarded. Jesus does not mean that if you work hard, sacrifice worldly pleasures, and try to withdraw your consciousness to the eye center, you will not be paid enough. Whosoever follows the teachings of a Saint and is sincere in his meditation will definitely get the reward, the wages of his meditation—and what is that?— "fruit unto life eternal," fruit that will give you eternal life. In our present state, after every death we have to face birth again, and the moment we come into the flesh, death starts dancing before our eyes. So he says: If you are able to lift up your consciousness to the eye center, you will be in touch with that Spirit, and once you are in touch with that Spirit, you will get the fruit, or the real wages of your meditation. Then the soul becomes pure, then nobody can pull you back to the creation.

Now we are attached to the creation, and these attachments are always pulling us to their own level.

When we are attached to the Spirit, the Spirit will detach us from everything in this creation. That Spirit will pull us out of the creation and take us back to the Creator. He says: This is the wage that is waiting for you, provided you put sincere effort into your meditation. You will get eternal life, "that both he that soweth and he that reapeth may rejoice together." He says: You will be happy that you have saved yourself from this miserable world, and the Master will be happy that his allotted work is finishing. Naturally, a professor is always happy to see his student shine in class.

> I sent you to reap that whereon ye bestowed no
> labour: other men laboured, and ye are entered
> into their labours.   *(4:38)*

He says: People are working very hard in search of the Father. They go to high mountains; they live in monasteries, away from their families, away from the world. They work so hard, but they get nothing in return because they know not what they worship *(4:22)*. You know what you have to worship. You know the method of worshipping the Father and you have not labored for this knowledge. I have given you this knowledge. Do not think that you have searched for me and found me. Actually my Father has drawn you to me. But for my Father, you would never have known anything about me.

5

Saint John tells us that when Jesus was in Jerusalem, at the pool known as Bethesda, he came upon a man who had been suffering from an infirmity for thirty-eight years. Jesus said to him, "Rise, take up thy bed and walk" *(5:8)*. And the man immediately did so.

> Afterward Jesus findeth him in the temple, and
> said upon him, Behold, thou are made whole:
> sin no more, lest a worse thing come unto thee.
> *(5:14)*

When a Master baptizes, or initiates us, we are in the process of becoming whole. He attaches us to the Spirit within, and when we are able to withdraw our attention to the eye center and keep ourselves attached to the Spirit, then we are on our way to becoming whole. Now we are not whole, because the soul is being dominated by the mind. The mind is a slave of the senses, and whatever the mind—as the slave of the senses—does, the soul has to face the consequences.

Whatever karmas or sins we have committed in this life and collected in past births will be washed away when we keep ourselves attached to the Spirit; and we should not add more to our karmas—"sin no more." But if we continue to cut other people's throats or kill animals for our food—or worse, for sport—we will have to come back to pay for these sins. Then the sins become our master and we become the slave, so we have to shift from body to body and thus become a victim of birth and death, which is "a worse thing."

When, by attaching ourself to the Spirit, all coverings are removed from the soul and the soul is released from the clutches of the mind, only then does the soul become whole. To "become whole" is the same as "know thyself," because the real self is the soul. So long as the mind dominates the soul, we do not know our "self." To become perfect, pure, whole—all mean the same thing.

Christ says: Now you are in the process of becoming whole, provided you "sin no more." You must not compromise with the four principles of Sant Mat. You must build your treasure in heaven on these principles. There are always rules to every game, so if you want to achieve results in meditation, you must be very strict in observing its discipline. You must build your meditation on a strong foundation, which is the principle told to us at the time of initiation.

Every day we remove dust from our house; and then if we do not close the doors and windows, more dust will come in. We will have to keep cleaning again and again, every day. So we remove all the dust that has gathered and close all the doors and windows so that more dust may not come in. Then our house remains clean. That is why Christ says: By attaching yourself to the Spirit, you will become pure; but do not be tempted by the senses again. Remain strictly committed to the principles of Sant Mat, "lest a worse thing come unto thee." As has been pointed out, the "worse thing" is that we may become a victim of birth and death, over and over again.

The Jews were angry and sought to slay Jesus, not only because Jesus cured the man on the Sabbath day but also because he said that God was his Father, thus "making himself equal with God." But he said to them:

> Verily, verily, I say unto you, The Son can do nothing of himself, but what he seeth the Father do: for what things soever he doeth, these also doeth the Son likewise. *(5:19)*

He says: I myself do nothing. I am not doing anything for my fame or glory. I do nothing, I know nothing. I do only what my Father wants me to do.

> For the Father loveth the Son, and sheweth him all things that himself doeth: and he will shew him greater works than these, that ye may marvel. *(5:20)*

Jesus says: My Father loves me because I am His obedient and therefore His beloved Son. I do only what He wants me to do—that which pleases Him. I always remain within His will. Just as a father gives anything asked by his beloved son, so He gives me everything. Anything I do which makes you marvel is really all His doing.

> For as the Father raiseth up the dead, and quickeneth them; even so the Son quickeneth whom he will. *(5:21)*

"Dead" means those who have absolutely forgotten the Father, those who are just living for the creation, those who have never, even in a dream, thought about the Creator. They are all dead people. Though they are breathing, they are dead. We are all dead as long as our

attention remains below the eye center, at the level of
the senses. But Christ says: The Father can fill even a
"dead" person with love and devotion, and the same
power my Father has given to me. My Father will not
come to your level to raise you from the dead; He has
given me that power.

Here I would also like to explain what is really
meant by the deaf, the blind, the lame, and the dead.
While it is certainly true that these physical conditions
were miraculously cured, and even the dead were
brought back to life by Christ and other Masters when
they saw fit to do so, these are not the real miracles.
Actually, until our soul is released from the domination
of the mind and senses, we are all spiritually deaf, blind,
lame, and even dead. It is the Master who brings us
back to eternal life by giving us the Word, the Nam, the
Shabd. It is he who enables us to walk on the path, to
hear the Word, the Celestial Music, the Sound Current.
It is he who enables us to regain our spiritual sight so
that we may see that Light within.

If Jesus and other Masters cured only physical ills,
they would be no more than great physicians, because
the physical body is perishable and has to merge back
into the elements of earth, water, fire, air, and ether at
the allotted time. The physical body was never meant to
endure forever. But the soul is immortal and can never
be happy until it returns to its source, the Father in
heaven. This is what Masters do for us, and therein lies
their greatness.

> For the Father judgeth no man; but hath com-
> mitted all judgment unto the Son: *(5:22)*

> That all men should honour the Son, even as
> they honour the father. He that honoureth not

> the Son honoureth not the Father which hath
> sent him.   *(5:23)*

The Father himself will never come to your level to make you worthy of Him. Unless you become worthy of Him, unless you become clean—that is, get rid of the load of your karmas—you will never be able to go back to Him. And the Father has committed that judgment to me; He has sent me to your level so that I may make you worthy of Him. That is why you should hear me attentively.

If you have no faith in me, then you have no faith in the Father. If you honor me, you are honoring the Father who has sent me. If you follow my teachings, you are following the teachings of my Father, and you are living the way that pleases my Father. Then you become worthy of the judgment of the Son and thus of the Father, because the Father and I are one. You become clean, whole, and only then can you become one with the Father.

"He that honoureth not the Son, honoureth not the Father which hath sent him." Christ says: If you do not heed my advice, if you do not respect me, if you do not follow my teachings, then actually you have no respect or love for the Father. If you have love for me, then automatically you will have love for the Father, because only through love for me, and love for the teachings which my Father has entrusted to me to share with you, can you become worthy of the love of the Father.

"Judgment" means to become worthy of the judgment of the Father; and to become worthy of the judgment of the Father means to become clean, whole, and rid of all the karmas which you have collected, because everybody is judged at the time of death according to the karmas, or actions, committed during life.

If you have been able to clear all your karmas and have become clean and whole, you become worthy of the judgment of the Father—worthy to become one with Him. And this you can achieve only through me, because the Father has entrusted this "judgment" to me. If one still has a karmic load at the time of death, he has to come back to this creation in one form or another. My Father has given me the privilege to make you worthy of the judgment of the Father. Judgment will be done by the Father, but whether one has become worthy of His judgment, that is to be done through me.

> Verily, verily, I say unto you, He that heareth my word, and believeth on him that sent me, hath everlasting life, and shall not come into condemnation; but is passed from death unto life. *(5:24)*

Who will get everlasting life? Who will rise above the grave? Those who are fortunate enough to be attached to the Word, or Spirit within, and have been able to build faith and love for the Master, will enjoy everlasting life, eternal life.

"Heareth my word" means to hear the Word, the Shabd, *through* me, the living Master. Our Master is the only one competent to take us back to the Father.

"And shall not come into condemnation." Now we are all condemned. What is this condemnation? To remain separated from the Creator. What greater condemnation can there be? So Christ says: You will have to face condemnation if you do not keep yourself attached to the Spirit within.

"But is passed from death unto life." As it is now, before we are on the path we hardly get rid of one body

before we become the victim of another birth, according to our past deeds. But as soon as we are put on the
path, we are on our way to eternal liberation or salvation.

To pass "from death unto life," therefore, means
that while everybody has to face death, those who have
made progress on the path will never have to die again,
because they will never have to be born again. They
alone will get everlasting life after the death that ends
this life.

> Verily, verily, I say unto you, the hour is com-
> ing, and now is, when the dead shall hear the
> voice of the Son of God: and they that hear shall
> live.   *(5:25)*

Christ is explaining to the seekers: You have come
to me and are listening to me; you are attached to the
Word, or Spirit within; you live my teachings and have
faith in me. The time for you has come when "the dead
shall hear the voice of the Son of God." Who are the
dead? Those who have forgotten the Father, who are
living only for the world and are slaves of the sensual
pleasures. They are dead as far as the Father is concerned and alive as far as the world is concerned. So he
says: The time has come when those people who have
absolutely forgotten the Lord, will hear me, will become filled with love and devotion for the Father, and
they will live for the Father.

He says, "They that hear shall live." Those who are
able to hear the Voice of God within themselves and are
filled with the love and devotion for the Father through
me, will not die. They will live, which means they will
have to leave this body eventually, but they will not have

to take another birth to face another death. They will live with the Father forever.

> For as the Father hath life in himself; so hath he given to the Son to have life in himself; *(5:26)*

> And hath given him authority to execute judgment also, because he is the Son of man. *(5:27)*

Why should you be attached to the Shabd, or Word, through me? Because the Father is the Giver of life—the Word that was in the beginning; and He has given the same Word and life to the Son, so the Son is the Word also. The Masters never perish, because their real form is the Word; therefore they are not the victims of birth and death.

My Father has given me the privilege, the authority, to pass the same eternal life on to whomsoever I wish. When I put people on the path—initiate them by attaching them to the Word—when they hear the Voice of God within themselves and when they live my teachings, then, like me, they also have eternal life.

> Marvel not at this: for the hour is coming, in the which all that are in the graves shall hear his voice,   *(5:28)*

> And shall come forth; they that have done good, unto the resurrection of life; and they that have done evil, unto the resurrection of damnation.
> *(5:29)*

We have made this body a grave. Christ refers to this body as a grave because only the dead lie in a grave. Those people who always live below the eye center and are slaves of the senses, Christ says, are all dead people; though they are living in the body and are breathing, they are actually living in a grave. He says: For them I have come. The time has come when they will no longer live in a grave. With my help they will withdraw their consciousness to the eye center and will hear that Spirit, or Word of God within themselves. The moment they come back to the eye center and attach themselves to the Word within, they are no longer dead. Then the body becomes the temple of the living God, because they become aware that He is within them and they are on their way back to Him.

And those who are attached to the Word, the Nam within their body, at the time of their death will be resurrected unto everlasting life. Others will become the victims of their own karmas, their sins, and will have to face death, again and again. So he says: Do not worry. When you live my teachings, you will automatically rise above this grave. You will not remain below the eye center.

> I can of mine own self do nothing: as I hear, I judge: and my judgment is just; because I seek not mine own will, but the will of the Father which hath sent me.   (5:30)

He says: It is not in my discretion that this person I make worthy of the Father or that person I refuse to make worthy of the Father. I of my own will do nothing. "I hear, I judge." Whatever my Father tells me, only that I do because I have no will of my own. I have merged my will in the will of my Father. So only those people will be able to rise above the grave whom He wants me to help, and those whom He does not want me to help will remain dead.

> If I bear witness of myself, my witness is not
> true.   *(5:31)*

> There is another that beareth witness of me; and
> I know that the witness which he witnesseth of
> me is true.   *(5:32)*

> Ye sent unto John, and he bare witness unto the
> truth.   *(5:33)*

Only a true Master can recognize another true Master; and John, having baptized, or initiated Jesus, bore witness that Christ was also a true Master.

> But I receive not testimony from man: but these
> things I say, that ye might be saved.   *(5:34)*

People asked him the question: How can we be sure that whatever you are telling us is good? How can we be sure that if we follow your teachings, we will be able to save ourselves from condemnation? Christ says: I have no witness to cite, so naturally you do not believe in me. Unless a statement is corroborated by two or three witnesses, nobody puts any faith in that statement. You have to put faith in whatever I am telling you, so that you can rise above the grave, so that you can get eternal life even while being in the body.

And why should I give you a witness? Why should I try to prove that what I am saying is right? "I receive not testimony from man." I am not trying to convince you so that I may become famous. "But these things I say, that ye might be saved." I am only concerned about you. Only on compassionate grounds am I trying to persuade you to have faith in me and to live in my teachings. Otherwise, you will never save yourself from birth and death. Then he talks about John the Baptist:

> He was a burning and a shining light: and ye
> were willing for a season to rejoice in his light.
>   *(5:35)*

Since John the Baptist had been beheaded and had finished his mission in this world, Jesus speaks of him as every Master speaks of his predecessor, as "a burning and a shining light." You were privileged to be in his presence "for a season" and to derive all the benefits and happiness of that association. A season has a beginning and an end; "for a season" means for a particular time, for a short period.

Christ is emphasizing that you could rejoice in John the Baptist's light only during his lifetime—he cannot help you now. Christ is saying this because some seekers who had never seen him were still looking to John the Baptist to guide them after he had been beheaded. Christ is impressing upon them the greatness of John the Baptist, but also warning them that he will not be able to guide them now, because that season is over. A Mystic can guide people in the world only as long as he is in the flesh.

No doubt John the Baptist was a great Mystic because he "came from God" and was the master of Jesus, having initiated (baptized) him. As a result of that initiation, Jesus had direct access to the Father, and in no way intended to minimize his Master's greatness.

A Mystic initiates only as long as he is in the flesh, but after his departure he is as far away from the seekers as the Father himself, with whom they cannot have direct contact until they have been initiated, or baptized. But once a Master has initiated a person, he never leaves him and is always with his disciple, whether he is still in this world or not.

What Christ indicates is that we always need a living Master to put us on the path. Without him we can never escape from birth and death. The necessity of the Master is from only one point of view: The Master can be at our level and also at the level of the Father. If he were only at the level of the Father, then why not worship the Father direct? He says: John the Baptist and Moses could lead you out of the darkness as long as they were living, but they have done their allotted work and have merged back into the Father.

> But I have greater witness than that of John: for the works which the Father hath given me to finish, the same works that I do, bear witness of me, that the Father hath sent me.   *(5:36)*

Besides my own Master, my deeds—the works that the Father has sent me to do—bear witness of me. By spreading the teachings given to me by my Master, I am also trying to keep that torch lit and to show you that Light. Then, when you have been saved, I can cite you as a witness.

> And the Father himself, which hath sent me, hath borne witness of me. Ye have neither heard his voice at any time, nor seen his shape. *(5:37)*

I have only two witnesses: My first witness is John the Baptist, who put me on the path and who commanded me to keep the torch burning, to show the Light to the seekers. The other witness is my Father, because He sent me. You know neither John the Baptist, because he has been beheaded, nor my Father, because

you cannot reach Him unless I put you on the path. So
there is no use in my citing any witnesses.

> And ye have not his word abiding in you: for
> whom he hath sent, him ye believe not. *(5:38)*

He says: Since you are not in touch with the Spirit,
or Word of God, within yourself, my citing the Father as
a witness is of no use to you, because only with the help
of the Spirit can you go back to the Father and inquire
from Him whether or not my statements are true. Then
he says: But I cite another witness.

> Search the scriptures; for in them ye think ye
> have eternal life: and they are they which testify
> of me.   *(5:39)*

The belief is prevalent in practically every religion
that by reading the scriptures we will be saved. But
unless we practice what is written in them, how can we
be saved? So Christ says: Thoroughly search the scriptures of the past Masters or Mystics with an unbiased
mind. Go deep into their teachings and you will find that
they tell you all about me. The scriptures of every religion will tell you about the teachings of the Saints—
that you have to go to a living Master if you want to
attain God-realization. Thus the scriptures are also my
witness.

But, he says, do not think you will get eternal life just
by reading the scriptures. You must do what they teach.
They tell you to find a living Mystic, so you must go to
one and follow him.

> And ye will not come to me, that ye might have
> life.   *(5:40)*

> I receive not honour from men.   *(5:41)*

> But I know you, that ye have not the love of God
> in you.   *(5:42)*

> I am come in my Father's name, and ye receive
> me not: if another shall come in his own name,
> him ye will receive.   *(5:43)*

He says: Strange is the world. We give so much love
and consideration to people who come to us for their
own fame. We bow before the kings, the rulers, the
wealthy people. We pay attention to them, we all show
respect to them. To people in authority we are always
obedient, because led by their ego they seek honor, and
because we are selfish we want some gain from them.
But Mystics come just for us. They want nothing in
return from us. They do not want to fill their pockets,
nor do they want to rule this world, nor do they want or
accept any gifts in return. They are concerned about
our spiritual welfare and want to save us from birth and
death, but we pay no heed to them; instead, we crucify
them. We cause them all sorts of trouble and hardships.
Christ says: I want nothing from you. I want *your* good,
and yet you are not paying any attention to me. You
want me to bring you two or three witnesses to convince
you that whatever I am saying is true.

> How can ye believe, which receive honour one
> of another, and seek not the honour that cometh
> from God only?   *(5:44)*

How can you even think of God when you are
steeped in flattery of worldly personalities? The honor
that you give to one another is false and meaningless.

Real honor comes from God, and that we can get only
when we honor the Son of the Father and through him
go back to our true home, the Father in heaven.

> Do not think that I will accuse you to the Father:
> there is one that accuseth you, even Moses, in
> whom ye trust.   *(5:45)*

Do not think that if you will not pay any attention to
my teaching, I will complain against you to my Father,
says Christ. I will never accuse you. Moses will accuse
you even though you think you are his disciples. He laid
down certain principles, certain commandments for
you to follow, as he was directed to do by the Father
during his lifetime. But you do not follow them. He
taught that you should follow a living Master; so if you
did follow his teachings, you would come to me. In this
way Moses himself is accusing you, if only you could
understand his teachings.

If you had faith in Moses and all Masters of the past,
you would have faith in me and would follow my teachings, Christ tells them, because every Master tells us
that we must go to a living Master. It is only through the
path given to us by a living Master that we can go back
to the Father. This is clearly stated in all scriptures,
including the Bible. Then he says:

> For had ye believed Moses, ye would have be-
> lieved me: for he wrote of me.   *(5:46)*

Not that Moses wrote anywhere about Christ—
"wrote of me" means he wrote about the necessity of
the living guidance to go back to the Father. So he says,

Moses is accusing you because he has made very plain
the necessity of the Master.

> But if ye believe not his writings, how shall ye
> believe my words?   (5:47)

He says: You read his writings, and profess faith in
Moses, but you have no faith in him. If you had faith in
Moses and in his writings, the scriptures, you would
definitely follow his teachings. If we have faith in the
Bible, if we have faith in Christ, we must live the teach-
ing of the Bible. Not that just by reading the Bible will
we be able to go back to Christ or say that he is our
Master—unless we follow what Christ has said in the
Bible, we are not the disciples of Christ. We are only the
disciples of our own mind.

So he says: Every Mystic has clearly written of the
necessity of the living Guide. If we want to become a
disciple of those Masters, we must follow their teachings. By our own efforts we can never go back to the
Creator; we have to look for somebody who has come
from the Father.

6

Then Jesus went over to the sea of Galilee, and a great crowd followed him.

> Verily, verily, I say unto you, Ye seek me, not
> because ye saw the miracles, but because ye did
> eat of the loaves, and were filled.   *(6:26)*

No doubt Christ performed miracles, but that was not the purpose of his coming to this world. No Mystic comes to this world to perform miracles. Their main purpose in coming into the flesh is to fill us with love and devotion for the Father, to put us on the path, and to help us go back to the Creator; but they are so kind-hearted, so compassionate, and so loving that miracles do happen in their lifetime. I do not deny that Christ performed miracles, but he did not perform as many miracles as are attributed to him. Many miracles have been added in order to show the greatness of Christ; and many things that happened coincidentally, probably we think were miracles.

Christ is telling a seeker: You are not attracted to me because you were impressed by the miracles I have performed. You have been drawn to me because you are filled with the "loaves"—you are filled with love and devotion for the Father. What he means to say is that we should be drawn to a Saint not because he can perform miracles but only because we feel the separation of the Father and want to go back to Him.

He says: Never go to a Mystic to get worldly favors, worldly honors, or worldly achievements, which you will ultimately leave in this world. Go to him for that which you cannot get anywhere else in this world. He says: What is that? That bread—Word—which can give you peace of mind while you are here in the flesh and which can draw you back to the Creator.

A conviction based on public miracles is shallow and short-lived. We should be so absorbed in love and devotion for the Father that this external evidence has no influence on our faith.

Christ did perform a few miracles, and when it became widely known that he could perform miracles, all sorts of people were drawn to him. They came from Jordan, Syria, Israel. When Christ saw the multitude, it is written that he went up a mountain and delivered the "Sermon on the Mount." His purpose was to give them the sermon explaining his teachings and to fill them with love and devotion for the Father. If you read the Sermon on the Mount, you do not find anything about the miracles in that. He is only telling us how to pray to the Father, how to give things in charity, how to forgive people, how to ask forgiveness of the Father, how to meditate, and how to be in touch with the Spirit. He did not perform any miracles while he was on the mount, and before that he used miracles only to attract people to him so that he could then teach them.

Then Christ explains to those people who were running after him only for the worldly "food":

> Labour not for the meat which perisheth, but for that meat which endureth unto everlasting life, which the Son of man shall give unto you: for him hath God the Father sealed.   (6:27)

He says: Generally we run after Saints for the fulfill-
ment of worldly ambitions. Christ asks his disciples,
Why do you want to collect worldly things? He explains: No matter how much wealth you may collect, no
matter how much authority or power you may have in
this creation, ultimately you have to leave it. Why collect those things which you are ultimately going to
leave? Why are you not contented with what the Lord
has given you? Why are you asking me for more and
more of the worldly things?

Do not ask a Mystic for anything of the world, "but
for that meat which endureth unto everlasting life." He
says: Go to a Saint to get that wealth which is your
property here while you are in the flesh and which is
your property even when you go back to the Father—
that spiritual treasure which will give you peace here
while in the body, which will make you the richest
person in the world, which will make you the king of
kings (meaning, which will make you one with the Father). "Which the Son of man shall give unto you." He
says: That thing only the Son of the Father can give you.
All other things you can get even from the worldly
people. A king can give you wealth and honor, but you
have to go to a Mystic to get that thing which you cannot get from anywhere else in the world—and what is
that?—the Shabd, Nam, Word, Spirit, the Voice of God
that is within every one of us.

Why do we have to go to a Mystic to get that treasure? "For him hath God the Father sealed." He says:
The Father has given him the authority to deliver that
spiritual treasure to you. In those old days, when a
court or a king issued an order, his own seal was used to
stamp the paper that carried the order. Without that seal
it had no authority. Similarly, Christ says, there is no

dearth of evolved souls in this world, but you can get the spiritual treasure only from that soul who has been "stamped," or "sealed," by the Father, one who has been appointed by the Father. Not everyone who has attained the state of God-realization is qualified to teach. There may be many who have reached that stage, but only the appointed or "sealed" Master can take us back to the Father.

> Then said they unto him, What shall we do, that we might work the works of God?   *(6:28)*

> Jesus answered and said unto them, This is the work of God, that ye believe on him whom he hath sent.   *(6:29)*

I am only doing the work of God, whatever He wants me to do. I try to create love and devotion in your heart for the Father, as He has authorized me to do. Others may have reached the same height spiritually, yet they may not be appointed by the Father to put others on the path. Only those marked by the Father are selected to put souls on the path leading back to Him. We are indeed fortunate to come across such a Master; but in reality, he is the one who is attracting us towards the path.

Not only are the Masters sealed by the Father, but the souls whom the Master is to initiate are also marked for that particular Master. He is to initiate only those souls who are marked for him. And each Master knows his own marked souls, just as a shepherd knows his own sheep. So that is what is meant by "this is the work of God." He marks the souls that are allotted to a particular Saint, and He also marks the Saint who is appointed to be a Master, a Son of God. Thus the Masters are doing the work of God in drawing those souls to themselves, and it is also the work of God that those particular souls believe in that particular Master.

> Verily, verily, I say unto you, Moses gave you not that bread from heaven; but my Father giveth you the true bread from heaven. *(6:32)*

This looks contradictory. At one point he says Moses is accusing you to the Father—it means Moses is at the level of the Father. And now he says Moses cannot deliver that bread from heaven to you. But it is not at all contradictory. He says: Moses cannot deliver the bread, the Word, from heaven to you *now*. Moses could deliver the bread from heaven when he was living in this world, but he has gone back to the Father long ago. Moses cannot deliver that bread to you—Moses cannot fill you with love and devotion for the Father, he cannot initiate you, he cannot lead you back to the Father *now*. "But my Father giveth you the true bread from heaven." He says: *That* bread you can get only through the grace of the Father. And what is His grace?

> For the bread of God is he which cometh down from heaven, and giveth life unto the world.
> *(6:33)*

He says: Only that person who has come from the Father to your level can give you the "bread" from heaven. To those fortunate ones who came to Moses during his lifetime, he gave the spiritual bread that ultimately took them back to the Father. But now Moses cannot deliver that spiritual bread. Without going to some living Master, you cannot get that spiritual bread from the Father.

> Then said they unto him, Lord, evermore give
> us this bread.   (6:34)

Now Christ talks about himself:

> I am the bread of life: he that cometh to me shall
> never hunger; and he that believeth on me shall
> never thirst.   (6:35)

This, of course, is symbolic and has a deep mystic meaning. This "bread of life" is the Word, Nam, or Shabd, which is the real form of the Master. No matter what you give the physical body to eat and drink, it will again become hungry and thirsty. Similarly, no matter what even God himself gives us in this world, we are not permanently happy nor contented with any worldly gift. We always hunger and thirst for more worldly possessions or power. But if we contact a Master and he accepts us into his fold and attaches us to the Word, we will then have absolutely no worldly desire left. We are never again hungry or thirsty. We will have only one desire: to go back to the Father. Then we will not go to a Mystic for any worldly boon. We will not want any miracles, because we will want only that "loaf" which can fill us with love and devotion for the Father. So he says: Moses cannot quench your thirst now. Now I can quench your thirst because I am at your level.

> All that the Father giveth me shall come to me;
> and him that cometh to me I will in no wise cast
> out.   (6:37)

He says: To whom am I going to give that bread? It is not for me to decide. My Father will automatically pull to me those to whom He wants to give that bread. I do not have to search for them. I do not have to advertise. They will be drawn to me automatically. They are already marked; they are already allotted to my care. I share that bread with only those fortunate ones.

"And him that cometh to me I will in no wise cast out." I have no authority to refuse those who are drawn to me by my Father. I cannot discriminate against those souls who are laden with very heavy karmas. I cannot leave them behind and take only the good souls back to the Father. Christ gives the beautiful example of a shepherd and his sheep.[1] He says: I have come as a shepherd, and the marked souls are sheep. The sheep belong to the landlord. The shepherd is only engaged by the landlord to look after the sheep, and to look after *all* the sheep—not only the good sheep, but also the bad sheep that sometimes go astray from the fold.

> For I came down from heaven, not to do mine own will, but the will of him that sent me. *(6:38)*

He says: I have no authority to refuse anybody; it is for the Father to do the marking. Whom He marks, why He marks, when He marks—is not for me to question. I am to deliver the "bread" only to those who have been drawn to me. Then he makes it still clearer:

> And this is the Father's will which hath sent me, that of all which he hath given me I should lose nothing, but should raise it up again at the last day. *(6:39)*

---

1. *John 10:1–18, 26–27.*

He says: My Father's command is that I should not lose a single marked soul to this creation, "but should raise it up again at the last day." My responsibility does not finish just by putting them on the path or by taking them into my care. I am also responsible to raise them "at the last day." "The last day" means the time of death, and everybody has his own last day. So at the time of their death I must come personally to receive them in my Radiant Form and I must lead them personally back to the Father. This is what my Father wants. Souls are lost in this world, and unless I lead them from this creation back to the Creator, they will never be able to go back to the Creator. But he makes a condition:

> And this is the will of him that sent me, that every one which seeth the Son, and believeth on him, may have everlasting life: and I will raise him up at the last day.   *(6:40)*

This is very important. Christ says: I am responsible only for those sheep who *see me* and who *believe in me*. When do we see someone? When we are both alive and at the same level at the same time. When the Master and the disciple are both in the flesh, then the disciple sees the Master. When the Master is not in the flesh, how can the disciple see the Master? Now, when we have never seen Christ in the flesh, how can we expect him to raise us at the last day? So he says: The first thing is that the soul must come to me when I am in the body.[1] The necessity of the *living* Master is the first fundamental condition in the teachings of every Mystic.

---

1. Initiation by the Master, whether personally or through proxy while he is in the flesh, fulfills the requirement of a "living Master."

And then, the disciple must believe in the Master, which means he should have faith in the Master, live and follow his teachings. You will withdraw your soul current to the eye center and you will hear the Voice of God within yourself. That is believing in a Mystic or following a Mystic. So the Master and disciple should, therefore, both be in the flesh. He says: Then I am responsible to raise you at the last day. If you have not seen me, if you have no faith in me, if you do not follow my teachings, then do not expect me to raise you at the last day.

But instead of groping in the dark and remaining in suspense about whether or not we will be met at the last day, we should work to see the Master's Radiant Form during our lifetime. Then we will know positively that we will be received at the last day.

> The Jews then murmured at him, because he said, I am the bread which came down from heaven.   (6:41)

> And they said, Is not this Jesus, the son of Joseph, whose father and mother we know? how is it then that he saith, I came down from heaven?   (6:42)

Naturally this was very hard for the disciples to accept, because they had known Jesus as a child and had been brought up in the same city. They knew his father, they knew his mother. So someone said: Who is this man who has been one of us all his life and now says that he has come from the Father, that he is "the bread of life" and he is going to share this bread which he has brought from heaven? Naturally all his associates started murmuring.

> Jesus therefore answered and said unto them,
> Murmur not among yourselves.　　　*(6:43)*

The people had their faith in Moses, in John the Baptist, or in Elias. They thought those past Mystics would lead them back to the Creator. They had always looked to them for help. It was therefore very hard for them to digest Christ's statement that only I can lead you back to the Father because you have seen me and you have been baptized, or initiated, by me. You have not seen Moses or John the Baptist, so they will not be able to help you go back to the Creator. Then Christ says: Do not murmur. I know it is very hard for you to accept this principle.

> No man can come to me, except the Father
> which hath sent me draw him: and I will raise
> him up at the last day.　　　*(6:44)*

Nobody will seek me unless my Father draws him and guides him to me. We say that we have found the Master, but it is the Master who has found us. Unless the Father draws and guides a soul to the Master, that soul will never be able to find the Master. My Father draws all the allotted souls to me and it is only they who will be raised up at the last day, not everybody. Then he says:

> It is written in the prophets, And they shall be
> all taught of God. Every man therefore that hath
> heard, and hath learned of the Father, cometh
> unto me.　　　*(6:45)*

"Taught of God" means those whom the Lord wants to know Him and follow His teachings—and *live* the teachings. Naturally, the teachings of the Father can come to us only through the Son of God the Father. The prophets of the past have also written that all the souls who want to go back to the Father must come to "me," because without "me" a soul cannot be raised up at the last day. And by "me" is meant not only Christ, but the living Master of every age.

> Not that any man hath seen the Father, save he
> which is of God, he hath seen the Father. (6:46)

Christ makes it quite clear that we cannot see the Father simply by accepting the Master of our time. But if we follow his teachings and carry out the spiritual practice—attach ourselves to the Word, or Spirit—then one day we will definitely see the Father. No one can see the Father unless he meets a living Master who has been sent by the Father. Only one who has seen Him and realized Him within himself can take the disciple to his true home. Such a one has been sent by the Father into this world to take the marked souls back to Him.

> Verily, verily, I say unto you, He that believeth
> on me hath everlasting life.   (6:47)

Christ again emphasizes that we should not only behold the living Master but that we should also have faith in him. When we have faith in him, we naturally follow his teachings. Then we will get "everlasting life."

> I am that bread of life.   (6:48)

What Christ is saying here is that as far as the true seekers are concerned, he is the "bread of life." They

must come to him and live the teachings if they want to
go back to the Father.

> Your fathers did eat manna in the wilderness,
> and are dead.   *(6:49)*

Those who attach themselves to the creation, to
worldly possessions, objects, and faces, are spiritually
dead. They have not found eternal life. So it is no use
praising our ancestors; they cannot help us. But he
says:

> This is the bread which cometh down from
> heaven, that a man may eat thereof, and not die.
>   *(6:50)*

But if you attach yourself to the Word—which is the
"bread of life" that I can give you, then you will not have
to come into this world again—you will have everlasting
life.

> I am the living bread which came down from
> heaven: if any man eat of this bread, he shall live
> for ever: and the bread that I will give is my
> flesh, which I will give for the life of the world.
>   *(6:51)*

He says, "I am the living bread," which means, only
I can deliver the bread that will give you eternal life, and
I have brought that bread from heaven. That bread
means the spiritual bread, not bread made of corn or
wheat. "And the bread that I will give is my flesh, which
I will give for the life of the world." He says: There is no
difference between that bread and my flesh. "My flesh"
means my essence which is that Word.

What gives life? Flesh and blood. We cannot live in this body without flesh and blood. Similarly, what is the flesh of Christ? What is the flesh and blood, or essence, of a Mystic? It is the Word, that spiritual bread, that Shabd, that Spirit, because *that* is the Master. The Master is not the flesh, though in a physical body he looks like us. The Master *is* "the Word made flesh." We have the Word in us, but we are not attached to the Word. We are not conscious of that Word, we do not hear it. The blood or the flesh of Christ is the flesh of that Word, the flesh of the spiritual body of Christ, not the flesh of Christ's physical body. He further explains this point:

> Then Jesus said unto them, Verily, verily, I say unto you, Except ye eat the flesh of the Son of man, and drink his blood, ye have no life in you.
> *(6:53)*

"Life" means the spiritual life. The people he was talking to were living. But, he says, you have no spiritual life. Though in the body, you are dead as far as the Father is concerned; actually we live when we live for the Father. Otherwise we are all dead.

> Whoso eateth my flesh, and drinketh my blood, hath eternal life; and I will raise him up at the last day.   *(6:54)*

Only those who eat my flesh and drink my blood will have eternal life, and only them will I raise at the last day. I will not come to raise everybody who professes that I am his Master.

> For my flesh is meat indeed, and my blood is
> drink indeed.   *(6:55)*

> He that eateth my flesh, and drinketh my blood,
> dwelleth in me, and I in him.   *(6:56)*

Now he makes it clear: Whoever drinks my blood
and eats my flesh merges into me and I merge into him.
We both become one. You lose your identity and become me. Now, how can our physical body merge into
the physical body of Christ? He says: Unless I merge
into you and you merge into me, you cannot go back to
the Father. How can those two physical bodies merge
and become one? What he is referring to is the spiritual
body, which is the Spirit, the Word made flesh, the
Radiant Form of the Master. The soul has to merge into
the Radiant Form of the Master. Only then does it merge
into the Divine Ocean forever.

> As the living Father hath sent me, and I live by
> the Father: so he that eateth me, even he shall
> live by me.   *(6:57)*

> This is that bread which came down from heav-
> en: not as your fathers did eat manna, and are
> dead: he that eateth of this bread shall live for
> ever.   *(6:58)*

Why does he say "living Father"? The Father is
always living, but for us He is dead because we do not
see Him anywhere. Christ says: My Father is always
living for me, because "I live by the Father." I am always
with Him. I have eaten the flesh and drunk the blood of
my Father, so I have become one with the Father. "So he
that eateth me, even he shall live by me." Since you are

not at the level of the Father, you cannot drink His blood and eat His flesh. I am at your level and have become one with the Father, so you can eat my flesh and drink my blood. If you merge into me, through me you will also merge into the Father. That is the reason the living Master is indispensable. The "bread of life" is the Word, or Spirit, which gives us everlasting life. The real form of the Master is also the Word, or Spirit—the Word made flesh. By attaching us to the Word, the Master also makes us one with the Word, and through him we merge into that Ocean of Spirit.

> Many therefore of his disciples, when they had heard this, said, This is an hard saying; who can hear it? *(6:60)*

When the disciples heard all this, it was very hard for them to hear and digest it. Jesus noticed that they were all murmuring at this, and said:

> What and if ye shall see the Son of man ascend up where he was before? *(6:62)*

> It is the spirit that quickeneth; the flesh profiteth nothing: the words that I speak unto you, they are spirit, and they are life. *(6:63)*

Now he makes it still clearer. He says: My real self is the Word, the Shabd, which is my Radiant Form. That is your Master. You have to merge into that Shabd, or Word. It will pull you back to the Father. From my flesh you will get nothing unless you attach yourself through me to that Spirit within. It is not the physical body of Christ that is going to take the disciple back to the Father. Christ and his disciples have left their bodies here, but when Christ was in the flesh and the disciples were in the flesh, they were at the same level. Then, through Christ's living body, the souls of those living disciples were brought in touch with the Spirit of the Christ, and that Spirit pulled those souls back to the Father. So the real disciple is the soul; the real Master is the Spirit in the flesh of the Master.

That Word dwells in us, and we ultimately dwell in that Word. Ultimately we merge into it, we merge into the Radiant Form of the Master. Only then we become one with the Master, and then through him we become one with the Father. So that is why he says, "It is the Spirit that quickeneth; the flesh profiteth nothing."

> But there are some of you that believe not. For Jesus knew from the beginning who they were that believed not, and who should betray him.
> *(6:64)*

> And he said, Therefore said I unto you, that no man can come unto me, except it were given unto him of my Father.   *(6:65)*

Many seekers are drawn towards the Mystics, but all of them are not meant to understand, accept, and live the teachings. Naturally Jesus knew who were the marked ones, who were the ones who were going to follow him; also, who was going to betray him and not follow his teachings. He said: My Father wants certain people to understand my teachings, and they will be made receptive to what I am saying. Only those who have been prepared for me by my Father will automatically be drawn to me, and will understand what I say, because they have been made receptive by my Father. Only they will understand and live my teachings, and it is only them I will raise at the last day. Nobody can come to me unless he is sent to me by my Father, and only he will understand the necessity of a living Master. They will live my teaching, and I will raise them at the last day—not everybody. Nobody can come to me unless he is sent to me by my Father.

7

After explaining how to worship the Father, and the necessity of a living Master, Jesus walked in Galilee, avoiding those who sought to kill him. As the Jews were about to celebrate the Feast of the Tabernacles, those who were with Jesus asked him to go to Judea, show himself to the world, and do his work openly so that he may be known *(7:1–5)*.

> Then Jesus said unto them, My time is not yet come: but your time is always ready.   *(7:6)*

This means that everything is destined according to the will of the Lord. Jesus says: I have come for a particular purpose, for an allotted period, and my time has not yet come.

Everyone comes into this world for an allotted period of time, according to his own destiny. One's own past actions in previous lives determine the type of life and span of life that he is to have in this world. Sometimes, as soon as a soul has left one body at death, it immediately enters the mother's womb at the time of conception. Sometimes there is an intermediate period of reward in paradise or punishment in hell before the soul again comes back into this world in some species of life, according to its karma, or destiny. This round of rebirth continues until the soul contacts a Master and gets attached to the Word within. Then it will never again go into a lower type of life, but will follow the spiritual path under the guidance of the Master until it merges back into the Lord and is forever liberated from the wheel of birth and death.

Christ came into this world for a particular purpose. Like John the Baptist and all true Masters, he was sent directly from God, and when that mission was completed he merged back into the Father. So he says that his task is not yet finished—his time has not yet come. But "your time"—the disciple's time—is always at hand. That is to say: Now is the time for us to take advantage of the opportunity of receiving the grace of the Lord through the Word, since we have been consciously connected to it by the Master. The Lord's grace is always there, ready for us; we need only to become receptive to it.

> The world cannot hate you; but me it hateth, because I testify of it, that the works thereof are evil.   *(7:7)*

> Go ye up unto this feast: I go not up yet unto this feast; for my time is not yet full come.   *(7:8)*

> When he had said these words unto them, he abode still in Galilee.   *(7:9)*

> But when his brethren were gone up, then went he also up unto the feast, not openly, but as it were in secret.   *(7:10)*

> Then the Jews sought him at the feast, and said, Where is he?   *(7:11)*

> And there was much murmuring among the people concerning him: for some said, He is a good man: others said, Nay; but he deceiveth the people.   *(7:12)*

Howbeit no man spake openly of him for fear of
the Jews.   *(7:13)*

Now about the midst of the feast Jesus went up
into the temple, and taught.   *(7:14)*

The world does not hate worldly people. They are
always given honor and praise. But they hate me, Christ
says, because I do not condone their bad deeds. Instead, I tell them that they should try to get rid of their
bad habits by rising above the sensual pleasures. I try to
give them something which is good for them and which
will take them out of this prison of illusion—the endless
wheel of births and deaths. But in their ignorance they
prefer to cling to the worldly pleasures. They do not
realize that howsoever great the pleasures of the world
may be, they are not only short-lived but also have unpleasant reactions at some time or the other. So they
hate me for trying to enlighten them and do not even
want to know about the eternal and everlasting bliss.

And the Jews marvelled, saying, How knoweth
this man letters, having never learned? *(7:15)*

This man is giving such beautiful mystic teachings
and yet we know that he has not had that type of education. How can he even know of such things, much less
talk about them? No Saint or Master obtains his knowledge by book-learning or formal education; he acquires
it by inner experience, by direct contact with the Father
through His Word—His Shabd, or Nam. He knows by
direct perception of the soul, without the medium of the
physical organs or the mind. History reveals that some
Masters have had practically no education, while others
had some, and still others had the best education that

this world could offer. But their learning or lack of it
had no bearing whatsoever on their spiritual knowledge, and this was also the case with Christ.

> Jesus answered them, and said, My doctrine is
> not mine, but his that sent me.   *(7:16)*

Jesus says: What I am trying to teach you is not my
own philosophy but belongs to the Father, who sent me
to teach you. If the teachings are from the Father, they
are ageless—older than history itself. They were not in-
vented by man; hence they were the same in the beginning as they are now and ever shall be. The method of
explaining the teachings may be different according to
the background of the seekers, but the actual teachings
are always the same.

Every Saint teaches the same path, the same truth,
which is always simple and direct. But after a Saint departs, the followers forget the real teachings and bind
themselves with various dogmas, rites, and ceremonies. Thus the teachings themselves are forgotten and
the people take the dogmas and rituals to be the real
path. Then the successor again revives the true teachings—that we should contact a living Master, get initiation from him, and under his guidance follow the path
back to the Father. The truth is just as simple as that.
This has always been the path and will always be. It can
never change, for it comes from the Father himself. But
only a few will listen and follow—only those who are
marked to go back to the Father. This is the way it
always happens. The Master's followers are comparatively few, but the followers of external rituals and ceremonies are many.

If any man will do his will, he shall know of the
doctrine, whether it be of God, or whether I
speak of myself.   *(7:17)*

When you will be able to live in the will of the
Father—when you rise above the realm of mind and
illusion—then you will realize whether I am giving you a
new teaching of my own or the teaching of the Father.
Until then you cannot understand this philosophy, for
you have to come to that level of consciousness to understand whether I am speaking for my own glory or
whether He that has sent me is speaking through me.

He that speaketh of himself seeketh his own
glory: but he that seeketh his glory that sent
him, the same is true, and no unrighteousness is
in him.   *(7:18)*

He says· If anybody tries to give a shortcut to go
back to the Father and tries to teach without being
authorized or stamped by the Father, he is only talking
for his own fame. Those who are seeking their own
glory will always remain part of the creation. I do not
teach for my fame, because I have no will of my own. I
do only what pleases my Father. I do not do anything to
please my own self.

Did not Moses give you the law, and yet none of
you keepeth the law? Why go ye about to kill
me?   *(7:19)*

Moses also gave you the same teachings, the law
that governs the return of the soul from the creation
back to the Creator, but "none of you keepeth the law."

You have forgotten his real teachings because Moses died long, long ago. You are being exploited by the interested persons, so you misunderstand his teachings. You have forgotten the worship of Spirit. You think you will find the Lord in the Sinai desert, in the mountains, in some synagogue or temple in Jerusalem.

"Why go ye about to kill me?" Moses told you not to kill any being—"Thou shalt not kill"—and you are thinking of killing even me. What have I done against you? I am only trying to fill you with love and devotion for the Father. I am only giving you the same old teachings that Moses gave you during his lifetime.

> . . . and I am not come of myself, but he that sent me is true, whom ye know not.   *(7:28)*

> But I know him: for I am from him, and he hath sent me.   *(7:29)*

I have not come into this world of my own accord nor for my own fame and glory. My Father has sent me, so whatever I do, I do in the name of my Father. I know that my Father has sent me, and my Father knows that He has sent me, so we both know that I am doing His work. But you have not seen Him and you do not know Him, so you will have to have faith in me if you want to go back to Him.

> Then they sought to take him: but no man laid hands on him, because his hour was not yet come.   *(7:30)*

> Any many of the people believed on him, and said, When Christ cometh, will he do more

miracles than these which this man hath done?
(7:31)

The Pharisees heard that the people murmured
such things concerning him; and the Pharisees
and the chief priests sent officers to take him.
(7:32)

Then said Jesus unto them, Yet a little while am
I with you, and then I go unto him that sent me.
(7:33)

When the people began to believe in Christ and to
follow his teachings, the Pharisees and the chief priests
could not tolerate this and arranged to send officers to
arrest him. It was not the Jewish people as a whole that
wanted to kill Christ, but the Pharisees and the chief
priests spread false propaganda and incited the mobs
until the Romans crucified Christ.

Christ knows that he will be crucified soon, so he is
explaining to them: Do not think I am going to live here
forever. I am with you only for a short time, for a
particular period, for a season. I am not going to guide
you for generations and generations to come. "And then
I go unto him that sent me." Then I go back to my
Father; I have come from Him to your level to guide you
to the Father, and after I have accomplished my task I go
back to Him. Then I have no business to be here in the
flesh.

Ye shall seek me, and shall not find me: and
where I am, thither ye cannot come.   *(7:34)*

When I am no longer in the body, you will all seek
me. You will hear about my glory. You will all claim that

I am your Master, but then you will not be able to make any use of my teachings because you will not have seen me nor will you have been put on the path by me. So there will be no link between you and me. It is only now that I can create this link. Now I can take care of you—not after I leave this body. "And where I am, thither ye cannot come." Once I go back to Him, you will never be able to reach me or to make use of the Light that is available to you now. I will be as far away from you as the Lord himself. So if we need a Master, it has to be a *living* Master. Otherwise he is as far away from us as the Lord himself. Then why not worship the Lord direct? What is the necessity of a medium if the medium is also as unapproachable as the Lord himself?

> Then said the Jews among themselves, Whither will he go, that we shall not find him? Will he go unto the dispersed among the Gentiles, and teach the Gentiles? *(7:35)*

> What manner of saying is this that he said, Ye shall seek me, and shall not find me: and where I am, thither ye cannot come? *(7:36)*

> In the last day, that great day of the feast, Jesus stood and cried, saying, If any man thirst, let him come unto me, and drink. *(7:37)*

He says: If you are thirsty, if you are yearning to merge back into the Father, you should come to me *now*. *Now* you should try to know my teachings and to live them. "Let him come unto me, and drink." Now you should drink that Nectar, that living water, which is within every one of us.

Day and night that Nectar is at the eye center, but your cup is upside down. Howsoever it may rain, not a drop can enter the cup. If you are able to turn the cup upright, one or two rains will fill it. Christ asks, When can you drink that Nectar? When you follow my teachings and withdraw your consciousness to the eye center, you will be one with the Spirit and see that Light within yourself.

You have thirst and hunger for the world. You have desires for the world. Whatsoever the Lord may give you from this creation, you can never be satisfied; but when you drink that Nectar of living water, you will not be thirsty anymore. When you are filled with that Light and Sound, you will have no desire for the world. Then nothing can pull you to the level of the creation.

> He that believeth on me, as the scripture hath said, out of his belly shall flow rivers of living water.   (7:38)

This is very beautiful. When do we believe in a Mystic? When we try to follow his teachings, when we change the basic pattern of our life according to his instructions. "As the scripture hath said" means the writings of every Mystic who came before me and explained the same spiritual truth. It is in your own scriptures if you will but read and understand them. Every prophet has been giving you the same law. If you go deep into the scriptures, they will tell you of the necessity of the living Master and of drinking that living water.

"The living water" is just another name given to the Divine Melody within and does not pertain to the water of this world. It is that Divine Melody, that Sound, that Light. So you can call it Nectar, Amrit, living water,

Divine Light, Holy Ghost, Spirit, Shabd, Nam, and by many other names. Muslims call it Abi-e-Haiyat. All these expressions mean the same thing.

"Out of his belly"—meaning out of his body—"shall flow rivers of the living water." He says: I am not going to put anything in you. The Lord has already kept that living water within everyone. You will not find it in synagogues, temples, churches, or mosques. You will find it only within yourself. And that living water is coming like water from a spring. As a spring never dries, that Nectar also never dries. Day and night it is pouring, but we do not withdraw our consciousness to that level where we can taste the Nectar and quench our thirst.

8

And early in the morning he came again into the temple, and all the people came unto him; and he sat down, and taught them. *(8:2)*

And the scribes and Pharisees brought unto him a woman taken in adultery; and when they had set her in the midst, *(8:3)*

They say unto him, Master, this woman was taken in adultery, in the very act. *(8:4)*

Now Moses in the law commanded us, that such should be stoned: but what sayest thou? *(8:5)*

This they said, tempting him, that they might have to accuse him. But Jesus stooped down, and with his finger wrote on the ground, as though he heard them not. *(8:6)*

So when they continued asking him, he lifted up himself, and said unto them, He that is without sin among you, let him first cast a stone at her. *(8:7)*

He says: We are very anxious to condemn others but we do not try to search within ourselves to see how filthy and how full of weaknesses we ourselves are. We always sit in judgment over others; we never try to clean the chamber of our own heart. If there is any one amongst you who has never committed any sin, let him

come forward and stone her. If you are as guilty as this
poor lady, then what right have you to punish her?

Whatever actions we do while we are in the flesh
become our destiny. But for that we would not be here.
He says: None of you is without sin. That is why you are
part of this creation. If you had no sin, you would have
been with the Father. How can you condemn this lady
when each one of you is full of sin? You should try to
help her rise above this sin rather than to condemn and
humiliate her. Mystics always find excuses to give us the
teachings.

> And again he stooped down, and wrote on the
> ground.   (8:8)

> And they which heard it, being convicted by
> their own conscience, went out one by one,
> beginning at the eldest, even unto the last: and
> Jesus was left alone, and the woman standing in
> the midst.   (8:9)

> When Jesus had lifted up himself, and saw none
> but the woman, he said unto her, Woman,
> where are those thine accusers? hath no man
> condemned thee?   (8:10)

> She said, No man, Lord. And Jesus said unto
> her, Neither do I condemn thee: go, and sin no
> more.   (8:11)

Why should a Saint condemn us? Saints do not
come to our level to condemn us—we are already condemned. To undergo the separation from the Father is
condemnation. What greater condemnation can there
be for the soul? Saints come to help us so that we may

not remain condemned forever. They come to help us to rise above our weaknesses.

Christ says to the lady: For whatever you have done, I do not condemn you. What is past is past. Do not worry about it; but *"sin no more."* Leave this type of life. What you have done in the past has brought you to the creation again. If you go on sinning like that, you will always remain a part of the creation. I will tell you the technique of getting rid of those sins. And what is the method Christ tells her?

> Then spake Jesus again unto them, saying, I am the light of the world: he that followeth me shall not walk in darkness, but shall have the light of life.   *(8:12)*

He says: As long as we are both in the world, I can show you the Light. We commit sins only as long as we are in darkness—and what is this darkness? In our body, the seat of the soul and mind knotted together is at the eye center. As long as the tendency of the mind is towards the sensual pleasures, we are all living in darkness, in ignorance. If you follow my instructions to withdraw your soul current to the eye center and see that Light within yourself, then you will be able to detach your mind from the sensual pleasures and enjoy the Light of life.

When you have diamonds, you will not run after shells. When you live in the Light, you will never choose to live in darkness. Christ says: Now you are living in darkness. That is why you are committing sins, but I will put you on the path and help you to rise above this darkness. "He that followeth me shall not walk in darkness, but shall have the light of life." Then you will

have that true Light, and when you see it within yourself, it will make you pure; it will give you eternal life.

> The Pharisees therefore said unto him, Thou
> bearest record of thyself; thy record is not true.
> *(8:13)*

> Jesus answered and said unto them, Though I
> bear record of myself, yet my record is true: for
> I know whence I came, and whither I go; but ye
> cannot tell whence I come, and whither I go.
> *(8:14)*

Christ has just said to the Pharisees: If you want to
walk in the Light, you must follow me. Now he says: I
cannot bring anybody forward to bear witness that I am
the Light of the world. Though what I say is true, I have
nobody here as a witness to convince you. I myself
know that I have come from the Father and that I am
going back to the Father after fulfilling my allotted task
in this world. But you cannot know whence I came and
whither I go, because you are living in the darkness of
ignorance and sin; you are a slave of the senses and of
your karmas. You have not penetrated this darkness
and seen the Light within yourselves, for if you had you
would recognize me immediately. So how can you understand what I am saying? However, if you want to
understand, if you want eternal salvation, you will have
to have faith in me—the living Master—and follow my
instructions.

> Ye judge after the flesh; I judge no man. *(8:15)*

When do we pronounce judgment over someone?
When we want to punish a person who has committed

an offense. Either he is acquitted or he is punished. So
Christ says: I have not come to punish you. I have not
come to judge what you do. I have come to help you to
rise above these weaknesses and go back to my Father.

> And yet if I judge, my judgment is true: for I am
> not alone, but I and the Father that sent me.
> *(8:16)*

But if I should judge people, my judgment is true:
for I can rightly judge because the Father and I are one,
and I know the past, present, and future. But I have
not come to judge you. I have come to save you.

> It is also written in your law, that the testimony
> of two men is true.   *(8:17)*

In ordinary law, two witnesses are always required.

> I am one that bear witness of myself, and the
> Father that sent me beareth witness of me. *(8:18)*

He says: I have no worldly witness to bring before
you. First, I am the witness of myself, and then my
Father is the witness who has sent me to your level, so
you can say that I have two witnesses.

> Then said they unto him, Where is thy Father?
> Jesus answered, Ye neither know me, nor my
> Father: if ye had known me, ye should have
> known my Father also.   *(8:19)*

Because he said, my Father is my witness, they
asked, Where is your Father? He says, "Ye neither

know me, nor my Father." You do not know the Lord.
You are worshipping only your own mental conception.
You are not worshipping the Father, because you can
never worship the Father unless you know the Son. So
he says, "Ye neither know me, nor my Father: if ye had
known me, ye should have known my Father also."
Only if you can recognize that I am the Son of the Father
can you know my Father.

> These words spake Jesus in the treasury, as he
> taught in the temple: and no man laid hands on
> him; for his hour was not yet come.   *(8:20)*

Christ knew when his allotted task would be finished
and when he would be asked by the Father to leave his
body, so he said that his hour was not yet come.

> Then said Jesus again unto them, I go my way,
> and ye shall seek me, and shall die in your sins:
> whither I go, ye cannot come.   *(8:21)*

I will leave you very soon and go back to my Father.
Then you will all seek me—"How I wish I could be with
Christ!" "Christ is my Master; I must follow his teachings." Then you will all profess your loyalty to me, but
now, when I am with you, you turn a deaf ear to my
teachings. You are still living in darkness. Once I leave
this body, you will not be able to reach me because I will
no longer be at your level. I will be only at the level of the
Father. History tells us that we always worship the dead
and persecute the living.

If you do not follow my teachings now, you "shall die
in your sins." Then you will not be able to get rid of your
sins. You will die along with the load of sins that you

have committed in this life and past lives, and those sins will drive you from one body to another body, from one "house" to another "house."

Both good and bad karmas are required for a human birth in this world. If we had all bad karmas we would be in hell; if we had all good karmas, we would reap our reward in paradise before again being sent into this world according to our destiny. This destiny, or fate, is carved out for us from our huge store of reserve karmas which have accumulated throughout the ages and from which a certain amount is taken as fate, or destiny, for each birth that we take. During each lifetime we per-form still more good and bad karmas, and these again determine our future destiny. So it is an endless chain. This is what is meant by saying that everybody is born in sin, or in other words, with his own particular fate karmas, or destiny.

> Then said the Jews, Will he kill himself? be-
> cause he saith, Whither I go, ye cannot come.
> （8:22）

The Jews naturally did not understand what Christ meant when he said, "Whither I go, ye cannot come." They thought probably he would commit suicide, but actually he was explaining—when I go back to the Father, then you will not be able to follow me to my destination.

> And he said unto them, Ye are from beneath; I
> am from above: ye are of this world; I am not of
> this world.　　　　　　　　　　（8:23）

You belong to this world because you are attached to this world; therefore you are "from beneath." This attachment leads you to commit sins which in their turn attach you all the more to the world, and bring you back to the world again and again in one form or another, because we always go where our heart is, where our attachments are. You cannot even be sure that you will always come back as a human being. But "I am from above." I am attached to my Father in heaven; that is where my heart is, so my attachment will take me to my Father.

If our attachment is with the Father, we will go back to the Father. But if we are attached to the world, birth after birth, we come back to the world. Any strong desires that remain unfulfilled or have not been sublimated, naturally create more attachments which form our future destiny. That destiny then enables us to fulfill those desires and, while doing so, we create still more attachments. But if we long to return to the Father, we will ultimately go back to Him. Because I am of the Father, because I am attached to the Father, if you follow me and become attached to me, you will go where I go— back to the Father. If you do not follow me and do not live according to my teachings, you will continue to be part of the creation in one form or another.

> I said therefore unto you, that ye shall die in
> your sins: for if ye believe not that I am he, ye
> shall die in your sins.   (8:24)

If you have no faith in me, if you do not follow me, you will have to "die in your sins." But if you have faith in the living Master, you will be attached to the Word, the Shabd, and then you can clear all your karmas and eventually return with me to the Father. But you must have faith in me.

Then they said unto him, Who are thou? And
Jesus saith unto them, Even the same that I said
unto you from the beginning.   *(8:25)*

I have many things to say and to judge of you:
but he that sent me is true; and I speak to the
world those things which I have heard of him.
                                      (8:26)

They understood not that he spake to them of
the Father.   *(8:27)*

There are many things that I could say to you, Christ
says, but you would not understand them. I tell you only
what my Father has told me and wants me to tell you.
Whatever my Father instructs me to explain to you, only
that much do I reveal to you. I do nothing of my own
accord.

Then said Jesus unto them, When ye have lifted
up the Son of man, then shall ye know that I am
he, and that I do nothing of myself; but as my
Father hath taught me, I speak these things. *(8:28)*

He says: It is very difficult to understand a Mystic.
You question, How can a man be God? How can a man
at our level be also at the level of the Father? Naturally
this doubt is in your mind. When will you be able to
digest this simple truth? "When ye have lifted up the
Son of man"—when you lift up your consciousness to
the level of the Son of man and see the Radiant Form
within; then you will know that I am the Lord in the
flesh.

You will have faith in me only when you see my
Radiant Form within; then you will know who I am.

Only when you have reached that stage within can you know that I am in the Father and the Father is in me, and what I am teaching you is true. Then you will know that these teachings are of the Father. You have all sorts of doubts when I am in the flesh like you. You feel that I cannot deliver you from this bondage, that only Moses or John the Baptist, who are no longer in this world, can deliver you. Now your faith is shallow and shaky; but once you lift up your consciousness to the level of the Master's Radiant Form within you, you will know that "I am He," that there is no difference between the Father and me. Then, even if the whole world turns against you, you will never leave me.

> And he that sent me is with me: the Father hath not left me alone; for I do always those things that please him.   *(8:29)*

> As he spake these words, many believed on him.   *(8:30)*

Do not think that my Father, after having sent me to your level, has forsaken me and I have become an orphan like you. He has not kept any veil between Him and me, but you will understand this only when you see the Radiant Form within—not before that. Although I am here, I am also with the Father.

I live only in the will of my Father. "For I do always those things that please him." I do nothing of my own will or for my fame. I live only to please the Father. I have risen above the realm of mind and illusion, and I have merged myself into the Father, so the Father is *always* with me. Then he elucidates further:

Then said Jesus to those Jews which believed
on him, If ye continue in my word, then are ye
my disciples indeed;   (8:31)

And ye shall know the truth and the truth shall
make you free.   (8:32)

He says: You should not think that you have become
my disciple and I have become your Master simply because I initiated you. To continue to be my disciple, you
must "continue in my word," which means you must
devote yourself to the spiritual practice that I taught
you—live a clean, moral life and do your meditation
every day. And you must continue your spiritual practice till your death. Meditation must become your way
of life, that is, not only to spend the allotted time in
meditation every day, but also to live according to the
principles of Sant Mat if you want to remain my disciple.
If you do this, then you are my disciple "indeed" and
will continue to hear that Word within. Then you are my
real disciple, my *real* lover.

Now you know only the creation, which is perishable. If you continue every day in the spiritual practice
as taught, and hear the Word within, then you will know
the Truth which is not perishable. And what is that?
That is the Word, the Shabd. Only that Word, that
Shabd, is the Truth. "And the truth shall make you free."
That Truth—that Word, or Shabd—shall make you
free from all your sins, free from birth and death. Now
you are attached to this creation, but when you hear that
Word, or Shabd—the Truth, which is everlasting—you
will have life eternal. Then you will get real comfort.

And what does Christ mean by "make you free"?
"Free" also means make you clean, whole, pure—all

these expressions mean the same thing. The Word, or Truth, shall make you free, make you repent for all your past sins, or karmas, and take you beyond the limits of mind and illusion. It also means that the Truth shall remove all the coverings from the soul, and the soul will shine in its pristine glory. The coverings consist of sins, karmas, mind, and illusion.

When the Pharisees heard Jesus say "the truth shall make you free," they did not understand what kind of freedom he was referring to. They protested that they were descended from Abraham and had never been in bondage to any man! They inquired of him:

> . . . how sayest thou, Ye shall be made free?
> *(8:33)*

Then, in the next three verses, Jesus explains his meaning:

> . . . Verily, verily, I say unto you, Whosoever committeth sin is the servant of sin.   *(8:34)*

> And the servant abideth not in the house for ever: but the Son abideth ever.   *(8:35)*

> If the Son therefore shall make you free, ye shall be free indeed.   *(8:36)*

There are two types of people in this world: those who are devoted to a perfect Master, and hence devotees of the Lord, and those who are devoted to the mind and senses. The devotees of the Lord always remain devoted to their Master and become free from sin by doing the spiritual practice as directed by him. The others are dominated by the mind and senses and have worldly values, which cause them to do worldly things, and this in turn causes an accumulation of sins and karmas—the chains that bind us to the material world—thus preventing us from going home to our Father in heaven.

Whenever we commit a sin, that sin becomes our master, and the soul becomes the slave, or "servant," of this master, because we must reap what we sow. Therefore, "whosoever committeth sin, is the servant of sin."

Further, Jesus says, the soul, as the servant of sin, cannot remain in the "house," the human body, forever, because we have only an allotted time to live in the body. Consequently, the soul must go where all the desires—created by the mind while living in this world—can be fulfilled or sublimated. In whatever body the soul is born, the same process of sinning continues, and the soul becomes ever more enslaved as a servant of sin.

Jesus says: I am free. I have no sins of my own, so I can also make you free like myself. Then you will be *really* free. Unless I help you, you will not be able to rise up, above the realm of mind and illusion. And how does the Master help us? He initiates us and thereby gives us a new birth. He reveals to us the technique of withdrawing the soul current to the eye center to hear the Spirit, the Voice of God, and to see the Light within. It is with the help of the Spirit and the Light that we are cleansed of all the sins we have committed, not only in this life but even in our previous lives. When the soul is cleansed of all the sins, it becomes free, and nothing can pull it back to the creation.

Thus the seeds of karma that the mind has sown can be nullified, setting the mind free from bondage. Only when the mind is free, or pure, can the soul become free from its bondage and return to the Father.

The "Son," on the other hand, is one who has risen above the sphere of sin, of action and reaction, and has become one with the Father. The sphere of action and reaction we call the realm of karma. And one who has risen above the realm of karma and become one with the Father is naturally saved from birth and death, and abides forever with the Father.

"The Son abideth ever" refers to any evolved soul who has realized the Father within himself and has merged into the Father. The master of the house can always go out of the house whenever he likes, but the servant cannot leave without the permission of the master. Our karmas are our master, but the Son is his own master.

We become master of our house, our body, when we are put on the path by a perfect Master, follow his instructions, and see his Radiant Form within ourselves. Since he is free from the bondage of karmas, when we contact him within and merge in him we will cease to be slaves of our karmas—"servants of sin"—and become master in our own house. Then "ye shall be free indeed," free from birth and death.

So if we want to become the master in this house, in this body of ours, then we must go to a Mystic, the Son of the Father, and he will make us free. When we follow the instructions of the Master with love and longing, and advance to the stage where we behold his Radiant Form within ourselves, he makes us free by gradually cleansing us of all our sins. Then we become master of the body and do not have to shift from one body to another according to the dictates of our karmas.

> I know that ye are Abraham's seed; but ye seek
> to kill me, because my word hath no place in
> you.   *(8:37)*

> I speak that which I have seen with my Father:
> and ye do that which ye have seen with your
> father.   *(8:38)*

The Pharisees were claiming a prominent and highly respected lineage—God-connected. Jesus, however, is characterizing them as godless because they have no real personal knowledge of God and do not even recognize Him when he stands before them in the human form.

Jesus says to them: I do only what I see my Father doing, and you people are doing the deeds of your forefathers. They used to kill and indulge in sensual pleasures. They were slaves of the senses. They were worldly people, attached to the world. Your worldly ancestors are your model; my Father in heaven is my model.

> They answered and said unto him, Abraham is
> our father. Jesus saith unto them, If ye were
> Abraham's children, ye would do the works of
> Abraham.   *(8:39)*

> But now ye seek to kill me, a man that hath told
> you the truth, which I have heard of God: this
> did not Abraham.   *(8:40)*

> Ye do the deeds of your father. Then said they to
> him, We be not born of fornication; we have one
> Father, even God.   *(8:41)*

> Jesus said unto them, If God were your Father,
> ye would love me: for I proceeded forth and
> came from God; neither came I of myself, but
> he sent me. (8:42)

Jesus points out to the Pharisees that though they claim that God is their Father whom they profess to love, they fail to conduct themselves as loving sons of God, because genuine Sons of God recognize one another and love everyone. But here Jesus has come from the Father who sent him, and the Pharisees do not recognize him and do not love him. Rather, they want to kill him for teaching what God has told him to teach.

And when he told them "this did not Abraham," he was telling them the same thing that he told others who claimed to be following Moses. Even if they had been sincere in trying to follow the teachings of Moses or Abraham, they were not actually doing so, for every true Mystic teaches that one has to follow a perfect living Master. As they were not living in the time of one whom they professed to follow and had no perfect living Master now, how could they be following the teachings of the one whom they claimed as their Master?

> Why do ye not understand my speech? even
> because ye cannot hear my word. (8:43)

Why do you not understand the simple truth: If you love the Father, you will also love His creation, because the Creator is within everyone. If you hurt anybody, you hurt the Creator in that person. It is a simple truth. You cannot understand my teachings and you cannot hear the Word, or Shabd, within because I have not attached you to it, but even this simple truth you do not understand. The question of killing does not arise when you say that you love the Father.

> Ye are of your father the devil, and the lusts of
> your father ye will do. He was a murderer from
> the beginning, and abode not in the truth, be-
> cause there is no truth in him. When he speak-
> eth a lie, he speaketh of his own: for he is a liar,
> and the father of it.   *(8:44)*

You do not understand my teachings, because you do not belong to me. You are worshipping Kal, the devil, the negative power; that is why you do not have faith in me. He has always been misguiding you from the time of creation, over and over again, birth after birth. He is a "murderer" of the truth because he is always deceiving you. You think you are worshipping God, but you are worshipping the devil.

If a person is sincere and honest in his devotion and really wants to worship the true Lord, then the onus is on the Lord himself to put him on the path. He will ultimately be led to a living Master and, receiving initiation from him, will follow the path to God-realization.

Jesus says: Kal—the negative power, or Satan—does not want me to show you the path. He does not want a single soul to go beyond his domain. He himself cannot create a soul, nor can he destroy one. All he can do is take an uninitiated soul out of one body and put it in another. But he is just. He rewards or punishes each soul according to the actions done by the mind. In this way he determines the destiny and life span of each body, and he also decides when and in what form each soul is again to return to this world. The whole cycle of life and death is within his domain, so his one object is to prevent every soul from escaping, because only a certain number are allotted to him and he will not get any new ones.

But when a soul is initiated by a perfect Master, it is the Master who takes charge of the destiny of that soul and guides it all the way home to the Father—sometimes in one lifetime, sometimes in two or three, but never more than four lifetimes. The Master sees to it that if the soul of his disciple has to take birth again, it will be in the human form and in such circumstances that will facilitate his spiritual progress. And he will have to be born again only if he has strong attachments that will bring him back into this world. Otherwise, after death, he can continue on the path in the inner regions and need not come back to this material level. That is why Kal fights hard to keep people away from the path, for he wants to hold them in the sphere of the mind and the senses. He is a liar, says Christ, but most people prefer to believe him instead of the teachings that will liberate them. Then he says:

> And because I tell you the truth, ye believe me
> not.   (8:45)

You are so blinded by the temptations of the negative power that you take his promises as true, and you do not believe me when I am really telling you the truth for your own good.

> Which of you convinceth me of sin? And if I say
> the truth, why do ye not believe me?   (8:46)

Which of you can prove that I am not of the Father? And since you cannot prove that, why do you not believe me? You have proof enough of your evil deeds and the temptations that beset you, right before your very eyes, so why not take to the spiritual path and save yourselves from all this misery? Make your own research and prove to yourselves that what I am telling you is true. I want nothing for myself. I only want to take you back to the Father. That is the only purpose of His sending me into this world.

> He that is of God heareth God's words: ye
> therefore hear them not, because ye are not of
> God. *(8:47)*

Only those belong to God—are on their way back to Him—who hear the Word of God, the Voice of God. But since you are not attached to the Word, or Shabd within, you do not belong to God; you belong to the world. You hear the voice of the world, you are in love with the world, so you will always remain in this world.

> Then answered the Jews, and said unto him,
> Say we not well that thou art a Samaritan, and
> hast a devil? *(8:48)*

> I have not a devil; but I honour my Father, and
> ye do dishonour me. *(8:49)*

When Jesus told the Pharisees that they did not hear God's Word because they were not of God, their closed minds and fixed worldly values and beliefs stood in the way of real understanding. They could see Jesus only as a threat to their economic interests, to their position of respect and authority in the community. In view of the popular interest created in his teachings, the only way they could think of dealing with him was to try to discredit him and vilify him by means of derision. They called him a Samaritan—someone from Samaria, whom the Jews considered a low human being—and they attributed his teachings as coming from one possessed by a devil. These remarks were intended to cause the people to view Jesus with suspicion.

"I have not a devil" means I am not of Kal, the negative power, but of my Father. Kal has nothing to do with me nor I with him. I know my Father and honor Him, but by not believing me you dishonor me and hence my Father who has sent me. If you will have faith in me, I can take you beyond the domain of Kal, back to the Father, where you will enjoy everlasting bliss.

> And I seek not mine own glory: there is one that
> seeketh and judgeth.   (8:50)

> Verily, verily, I say unto you, If a man keep my
> saying, he shall never see death.   (8:51)

This is something very beautiful. Which death will he never see? (Now it seems surprising, because even Christ had to face death. All his disciples are dead now. But he says: He will not see death *again*.) He will not face a second death. He will never be born again to face death again. So Christ says: If you live in my teachings, that is, withdraw your consciousness to the eye center and hear that Spirit within, you will not have to come to this world again.

> Then said the Jews unto him, Now we know that
> thou hast a devil. Abraham is dead, and the
> prophets; and thou sayest, If a man keep my
> saying, he shall never taste of death.   (8:52)

> Art thou greater than our father Abraham,
> which is dead? and the prophets are dead:
> whom makest thou thyself ?   (8:53)

After hearing Jesus say "If a man keep my saying, he shall never see death," and misinterpreting that as a promise to those who follow his teachings, of eternal life *in this very body,* the Pharisees seem to be gloating over what appears to them to be proof that Jesus, by his own words, is confirming their charge that he is possessed of a devil, if he is not the devil himself!

They argue that Abraham, the great patriarch and founder of the Hebrew nation—the beloved of God—is dead, and so are all the recognized prophets sent by God. None of them gave anyone everlasting life, and here Jesus is making such a promise. They ask: Are you greater than Abraham? Just who do you make yourself out to be?

> Jesus answered, If I honour myself, my honour
> is nothing: it is my Father that honoureth me; of
> whom ye say, that he is your God: (8:54)

> Yet ye have not known him; but I know him: and
> if I should say, I know him not, I shall be a liar
> like unto you: but I know him, and keep his
> saying.   (8:55)

He says, "If I honour myself, my honour is nothing." I do not do anything for my own fame. I am nothing. I am nobody in this world. I am the humble servant of everybody. It is my Father that honors me. My Father has given me the privilege and honor to be your Master. You say that the Father is your god, but your god is the devil, the negative power. Merely saying that you worship God does not entitle you to become His disciple or His devotee. Your words and deeds show that you do not worship God, though you profess to do so.

You do not know the Father, says Jesus. You say you love Him but you have never seen Him. How can you love or worship somebody whom you have never seen? But I know Him and have merged into Him and He into me. If I should say I do not know Him, then I would be a liar, like all of you who claim to know God but do not. I know my Father and I do exactly what he tells me to do.

> Your father Abraham rejoiced to see my day: and he saw it, and was glad.   *(8:56)*
>
> Then said the Jews unto him, Thou art not yet fifty years old, and hast thou seen Abraham?   *(8:57)*
>
> Jesus said unto them, Verily, verily, I say unto you, Before Abraham was, I am.   *(8:58)*
>
> Then took they up stones to cast at him: but Jesus hid himself, and went out of the temple, going through the midst of them, and so passed by.   *(8:59)*

The Pharisees were both shocked and amused to hear Jesus say that Abraham rejoiced and was happy with Jesus. They pointed out that Father Abraham had been dead for over two thousand years, and Jesus, who was not yet even fifty years of age, was claiming personal familiarity with him.

But Jesus was talking about the fact that Masters, having become one with the Father, know the past, present, and future. They are in this world and at the

same time they are with the Father. Masters, even of the
past, are with the Father, although they are no longer in
the physical body. And at the level of the Father, time
and space do not exist. So Jesus, having become one
with the Father, was also one with Abraham—and the
two thousand years that separated them in this physical
world did not exist. He was saying: Since I have become
one with the Father, so I existed along with the Father
before the creation—before even Abraham came into
this world in the flesh, I was. But now I am in the flesh at
your level, so in this world I have come after Abraham.
That is why you are surprised at my statement and feel
puzzled.

However, the Pharisees were totally ignorant of all
this, which accounts for their reaction when Jesus tells
them "Before Abraham was, I am." This they took to be
a claim by Jesus that he was God. Such "blasphemy"
could be dealt with only by stoning, but Jesus "hid
himself"—made himself invisible to them   and quietly
escaped from the temple to safety by simply walking
out through the midst of them.

9

And as Jesus passed by, he saw a man who was
blind from his birth.   *(9:1)*

And his disciples asked him, saying, Master,
who did sin, this man, or his parents, that he
was born blind?   *(9:2)*

The disciples of Christ wanted to know whether the
blind man was suffering because of his own sins or because of the sins of his parents. Christ gives a beautiful
answer:

. . . Neither hath this man sinned, nor his parents: but that the works of God should be made
manifest in him.   *(9:3)*

In the last chapter Christ had said, "I go my way, and
ye shall seek me, and shall die in your sins." If you do
not keep yourself attached to the Shabd, or Nam, you
will die along with your sins. Your sins will become the
master and you will become the slave. He is explaining
the same thing here—how sins are born along with a
person, how sins become the master and he becomes
the slave.

He says: In this life neither the parents have sinned
nor the child has sinned. How could the child have
sinned? He was born blind. He could not have sinned in
this life. So Christ says, "But that the works of God
should be made manifest." This fact proves the law of

nature, or the law of karma, the law that governs the soul from the creation back to the level of the Creator. Neither have his parents sinned nor has the child sinned, but they have all sinned in a past birth. For that, they are suffering now. The parents are suffering because they have to look after a blind child, and the child is suffering because he is blind. They prove the law of the universe, the law of karma, that whatever you sow, so shall you reap.[1] They have sown certain seeds in the past, and now they are facing the consequences of whatever they have sown.

A child is born an idiot or a lunatic; what has that child done in this life to suffer for? He must have done something in the past for which he and his parents are suffering now. We bring our destiny with us, and we have to face that destiny during our life.

Millions and millions of lives we have passed through, and in every life we have been collecting load upon load of karmas. How to get rid of these karmas now? How can the parents and the child help themselves to rise above their sins? He says:

> I must work the works of him that sent me, while it is day: the night cometh, when no man can work.   (9:4)

I can help you to get rid of all these karmas that you have brought along with you in this life. The Father has sent me to help souls who are miserable in this creation and yearn to go back to Him. The Father has marked them. To put them on the path and to lead them back to Him is my work, and I can accomplish my work only

---

1. "Whatsoever a man soweth, that shall he also reap" *(Gal. 6:7).*

"while it is day"—when I am in the body. "The night cometh when no man can work." When I leave this body, darkness will overtake you. Then I will not be able to put you on the path. He further clarifies this point:

> As long as I am in the world, I am the light of the world. *(9:5)*

Here Christ himself indicates that we must go to a living Master, for he expressly states that he is the Light of the world only as long as he is in the world. The seeker and the Master must both be in the human body at the time that the disciple is accepted by the Master. Once the seeker has been put on the path, it makes no difference whether the Master is still in the body and the disciple is not, or the disciple is still in the body and the Master is not, or whether they both have left the body. For the disciple, the Master who initiated him never dies, and his spiritual progress continues whether the disciple is in this world or the next, or whether the Master is in the flesh or has departed.

It is evident from Christ's own statements that those who have never seen him in the flesh and yet profess to be following him now are really mistaken. Christ never said that he would be the Light of the world forever. He said, "As long as I am in the world." He did not say that there would be no Light in the world after he left it. He says: As long as I am in the flesh I can show you the Light, but once I leave this body I cannot show the Light to anybody.

Thus, only through a living Master—who is the Light of the world during our lifetime—can we go back to the Father. The Father sends each Master into the world at an appointed time for those particular souls which were marked by the Father. Each Master is the Light of the world as long as he is in the world. If now we could go back to the Father through Christ, who has long since left the world, then there would never have been a need for any living Master or Christ to come into this world, because we could contact the Father direct. But we cannot contact Him direct, for the Father himself has ordained that we can go back to Him only through a living Master.

> . . . For judgment I am come into this world,
> that they which see not might see; and that they
> which see might be made blind.   *(9:39)*

It looks contradictory—how can a Saint even think of making us blind? But there is a beautiful mystic meaning behind it. He says: I have come to prepare you for the judgment of the Creator. Unless we become worthy of the Lord's judgment, we cannot go back to Him. And when do we become worthy of His judgment? When the soul becomes free from sins. Christ asks: And how am I going to prepare you? "That they which see not might see." Now we see only darkness, though the Lord is within every one of us and in every part of this creation. Christ says: I have come, that those people who "see not might see"—who do not see the Creator anywhere, are able to see Him.

Unless we see the Creator within ourselves, we cannot see Him anywhere in this creation. When we are able to open that eye which can see the Father within, our eyes are open to see Him in the world also. Then wherever we look in this creation, we see nothing but the Father. Then we know that the Creator is in every part of the creation.

"And that they which see might be made blind." You have eyesight only for the creation; I have come so that you will become blind to the creation, meaning, so that you are able to detach yourself from the creation. Then you will see the Creator everywhere in the creation and within yourself. Unless we are able to detach ourselves from the creation, we can see the Creator neither in the creation nor within ourselves.

A diamond necklace is always kept in a beautiful velvet box. If you take away the necklace, the box is useless. It has no value. So the diamond necklace enhances the beauty of the box. Without it, nobody wants to look at the box. Nobody bothers about it. You will just put it anywhere. But once you realize it contains the diamond necklace, you will place the box in your safe and will not even entrust your key to anyone. So when we realize the Lord within us, then we know the value of human beings, because they all "contain" the Creator. Automatically we become humble before them, we become respectful to them, we become loving and kind to them. Then they appear very beautiful to us. So long as we do not see the Creator in them, they do not seem to exist. They do not mean anything to us. So we have to realize that the Creator is within everyone, and not just by theory but by practical experience.

And some of the Pharisees which were with him heard these words, and said unto him, Are we blind also?   *(9:40)*

Jesus said unto them, If ye were blind, ye should have no sin; but now ye say, We see; therefore your sin remaineth.   *(9:41)*

We are at the level of the creation because we have
sins. If we had no sins, nothing could keep us bound to
this creation. The soul would automatically go back to
the Father. It is the weight of our karmas that is holding
the soul back in this creation. If you can become blind to
this creation—have no attachment to this creation—you
will have no sins. We have committed sins because we
are not blind to this world. Because we see this creation,
we are attached to this creation. We cannot detach
ourselves from the creation unless we attach ourself to
the Spirit within. Only this attachment can create within
us detachment from the world.

10

> Verily, verily, I say unto you, He that entereth
> not by the door into the sheepfold, but climbeth
> up some other way, the same is a thief and a
> robber.   *(10:1)*

What Christ means to say is that unless we find the
door to our own house, we cannot find the way in and up
to our true home. The door leading to our home of
eternal bliss is the third eye, and we can open it only
with the key that we get from the living Master, the true
shepherd. The shepherd has the key to the sheep pen
and he uses it to open the door, but thieves and robbers
do not possess the key—they try to climb over the walls
in order to plunder and lead the sheep astray.

The Master is our loving shepherd, and the eye
center, or the third eye, in our body is the door to our
house. It is through this door that the Master, in his
Radiant Form, receives his disciples and guides them
to the Father. By "thieves" and "robbers" is meant the
agents of the negative power, the false prophets, and all
those who mislead the people by preaching that salvation can be obtained through dogmas, rituals, and other
outward practices. It is only the true Master, the real
guide or shepherd, who can connect his disciples with
the Sound and lead them to the Father.

> But he that entereth in by the door is the shep-
> herd of the sheep.   *(10:2)*

Here he makes it plain that the Master, the true shepherd, in his Shabd Form, is always waiting for us at the door of our house. All we need to do is to knock at the door and we will be admitted by the shepherd, who will lead us to the Father. And this "knocking at our door" is done by means of the spiritual practice. We keep making the effort, and when we are fit to enter, the shepherd will open the door and receive us with open arms. He is there waiting for us and is longing for us to come, more than we are to go, no matter how strong we may think our urge to return to the Lord is.

> To him the porter openeth; and the sheep hear
> his voice: and he calleth his own sheep by
> name, and leadeth them out.   *(10:3)*

A shepherd calls his sheep; the sheep know his voice and will go to no other shepherd but their own. So it is with the Master and his disciples. Jesus explains that each Master recognizes the seekers who are marked to be his sheep, and every sheep marked for him automatically comes to him and has faith in him. The Master then leads us out of the prison of this world to everlasting freedom and peace—our heavenly home. He never calls us from behind, but is always in front of us. He remains ahead, always guiding and protecting us on the way.

The Master opens the door from inside, and the initiates then see the Radiant Form of their own Master. They are never deceived, for they have already seen him in his physical form, so they recognize him. "And he calleth his own sheep by name" means that he has called them and initiated them by giving them Nam, or Shabd—the Word, or Sound Current—through which he takes them back to the Father.

> And when he putteth forth his own sheep, he
> goeth before them, and the sheep follow him:
> for they know his voice.   *(10:4)*

This again refers to what we experience inside. As
we enter the third eye—the door leading to eternal
salvation—we see the real form of the Master and hear
his voice, the Sound Current, the Audible Life Stream.
And this Sound not only leads us but actually takes us
back to the Father. First we follow it; then as we make
internal progress, we merge into it and ride, or ascend,
to our home by means of the Sound, the Word. It is
constantly pulling us inside like a magnet and attracting
us homeward.

When we see the Radiant Form of the Master, we at
once recognize him, because we have seen our Master
outside in his physical form. If we have never seen the
Master, how do we know whether or not we are seeing the right shepherd? All the descriptions of Christ's
physical appearance are only hearsay. Even if he appears inside, how do we know he is Christ or somebody
else trying to project Christ's face? We have never seen
him. So that is why he says, The soul recognizes his
own Master because he has seen his Master.

> And a stranger will they not follow, but will
> flee from him: for they know not the voice of
> strangers.   *(10:5)*

Those who make a sincere effort, who are devoted
to their Master and have complete faith in him, will
recognize his Radiant Form within themselves. Of
course, Kal, the negative power, and his agents—who
are referred to as Satan and his devils in the Bible—will

try their utmost to lead a disciple astray by all sorts of trickery and temptations, even appearing to the devotee in the assumed form of his own Master. But the true devotee is not misled, because at the time of his initiation his Master tells him the method by which he can test whether the form he sees within is that of his Master or only a deception.

Thus the important thing for the disciple is to have absolute faith and confidence in his Master, or else he might forget to use the test and be temporarily led astray. But a true disciple pays no attention to the form or voice of strangers within, so he can never be misled.

> This parable spake Jesus unto them: but they understood not what things they were which he spake unto them.   *(10:6)*

Naturally, the simple people could not understand what Christ was trying to explain. Christ says that he talks in parables, so that only those who are meant to understand him will understand, while others who are not meant to understand may not.

> Then said Jesus unto them again, Verily, verily, I say unto you, I am the door of the sheep. *(10:7)*

He says: For my initiates, I will be at the door. I will be waiting for them at the eye center. The sheep has come to the door to be received by the Master. You have to withdraw your soul current to the eye center by means of the spiritual practice, and I am there waiting for you.

Unless the door is opened we can never enter a house. This is the door of the house Christ refers to when he says: Knock and it shall open.[1] It is the "door" at the eye center, and we have to knock by withdrawing our consciousness up to this point. Then the door will open to us from within, and we will find the way which leads us back to the Father. When we know the way, or path, and follow it, we will find the Father within, waiting for us, and will become one with Him. Unless we knock, the door does not open; unless the door opens, we do not know the path; and unless we follow the path, we can never find our destination.

> All that ever came before me are thieves and robbers: but the sheep did not hear them. *(10:8)*

Christ does not mean that all the Mystics and Prophets who came before him were thieves and robbers. What he means to say is that if you see anybody within apart from your own Master, no matter how great a Saint or Prophet he may have been in his lifetime, you may be sure that what you see is a thief and a robber. That form can be only a deception, an impersonation of the real Saint.

No Master, Saint, or Prophet of the past, including Christ, is going to appear before you now unless he is accompanied by the Form of your own Master. If you see anyone else within instead of your own Master, no matter how bright, pure, or saintly that being may appear to you, it is nothing but a deception, a trick of the negative power to lure you away from the path. Even good advice and predictions that come true will be given to you for some time by such impersonations just to gain your confidence; but do not be deceived.

---

1. "Ask, and it shall be given you; seek, and ye shall find; knock, and it shall be opened unto you" *(Matt. 7:7, Luke 11:9).*

A true disciple does not pay any attention to these appearances and does not listen to them, just as the sheep from one flock will not follow the shepherd of another flock, nor will they follow a thief who comes to steal them away. The Masters of the past have finished their work in this world and have merged back into the Father, so they will not appear before you in their Radiant Form unless they are accompanied by your own Master's Radiant Form. And you can always test these forms by using the method given to you at the time of initiation.

> I am the door: by me if any man enter in, he shall be saved, and shall go in and out, and find pasture.   *(10:9)*

He says: For my initiates, I am waiting at the door, which means that for them I am at the eye center. When they withdraw their consciousness to the eye center, they will find me there, they will see me waiting at the door. "By me if any man enter in, he shall be saved." He says: My initiate, if he meets me at the door within, will be saved from birth and death and from transmigration. "And shall go in and out, and find pasture." He says "pasture" because sheep are always happy to graze in a green pasture. Naturally the "food" of the disciple is the Radiant Form of the Master. Once you see my Radiant Form within yourself, he says, then at your own sweet will you can be one with the Master within and again come back to the body. You can go below the eye center whenever you want to, and you can be at my level and find me within whenever you want to. Then you can go in and out. Now you cannot go in at all. You are always out because your consciousness is always below the eye center.

> The thief cometh not, but for to steal, and to
> kill, and to destroy: I am come that they might
> have life, and that they might have it more abun-
> dantly.   *(10:10)*

Here Christ explains that Kal and his agents, or Satan and his devils, whatever you may call them, come only to steal, to kill, and to destroy. Do not let them deceive you and rob you of your spiritual wealth. It is true that what you have gained spiritually can never be taken away from you, but by forgetting the instructions of the Master and allowing yourself to be misled, you certainly invite unnecessary suffering and grief and may greatly delay your spiritual progress. So you should pay no attention to these thieves and robbers who come to you in the garb of your own shepherd, that is, in the form of Christ or of any great soul except your own Master.

Sometimes Kal may appear to you in your own form, trying to make you believe that you have reached the Father and that now you have become God the Father. But only your own Master can take you to Him. It is only he that can give you eternal life. "That they might have it more abundantly" means: Once you hear that Sound, Melody, or Shabd within yourself, it will go on increasing. The more you attend to it, the more it will increase. It will always be in abundance.

> I am the good shepherd: the good shepherd
> giveth his life for the sheep.   *(10:11)*

Like a good shepherd who always takes care of his sheep, the Master helps us clear our karmas, helps us wash away all the sins from our soul, until we are pure

and spotless and can merge back into the Father. He
alone knows what is best for us and regulates our progress according to our efforts and the karmas, or layers
of dirt, that cover our soul and mind.

First, the mind has to be cleansed so that it may
travel along with the soul to its own source or home,
which is Universal Mind, the second spiritual stage.
There the individual mind merges in the Universal Mind
and becomes happy. Only then is the soul free to go
to higher spiritual regions and eventually merge in the
Father.

Our Master, the good shepherd, helps us and looks
after us all the way. He always does what is best for each
individual soul. He even lays down his life for his disciples—he "giveth his life for the sheep"—by taking most
of their karmas on his own body so that the disciple's
load is light enough for him to bear. Even though we
may think we have a hard lot, it is but a small fraction of
what it would have been if we had no Master. Thus, not
only does he put us on the path but he also enables us to
travel on it by lightening our load of karmas.

> But he that is an hireling, and not the shepherd,
> whose own the sheep are not, seeth the wolf
> coming, and leaveth the sheep, and fleeth; and
> the wolf catcheth them, and scattereth the
> sheep.   *(10:12)*

> The hireling fleeth, because he is an hireling,
> and careth not for the sheep.   *(10:13)*

> I am the good shepherd, and know my sheep,
> and am known of mine.   *(10:14)*

Christ says: I am the good shepherd and know my
sheep, and my sheep know me. I shall not leave my

sheep, and if any of them go astray, I will myself bring them back to the fold. But the hirelings, the imposters, are not concerned with the sheep's welfare, so they are not interested in protecting them. When anything frightening comes along, they simply flee and leave the sheep without protection. But the Master never leaves his sheep, even though some disciples may go astray for a time. He is responsible to the Father for every soul allotted to him, and he himself brings every one of them back to the Father. But the sheep who do not belong to the flock of the Master are easily led astray by the hirelings.

You may have seen shepherds grazing their sheep. When a shepherd whistles, only his particular sheep go to him. There may be five thousand sheep brought together, and they may belong to three different folds and three different shepherds. When a shepherd whistles, only those sheep that belong to him will come to him; the other sheep will not listen to his whistle. That is why Christ gives this example.

> As the Father knoweth me, even so know I the
> Father: and I lay down my life for the sheep.
> *(10:15)*

He says: Why should initiates try to see my Radiant Form? Because I know the Father. They do not know the Father, so only through me can they go back to Him. "I lay down my life for the sheep." He says: I am willing to sacrifice *anything* to save the souls allotted to my care, because my Father wants not a single soul to be lost. I must bring every marked soul back to Him. This is my work. For this He has sent me to your level. I am prepared even to give my life to save them.

Christ has given a beautiful parable in Saint Matthew. He says: A shepherd has a hundred sheep. If one sheep runs out of the flock and down into the bottom of a ravine, the shepherd leaves the ninety-nine sheep and runs after that one sheep. He even takes that sheep on his shoulders and brings it back to the fold, because he is responsible for all the hundred sheep.[1]

> And other sheep I have, which are not of this fold: them also I must bring, and they shall hear my voice; and there shall be one fold, and one shepherd. *(10:16)*

What Christ is saying here is that I am also responsible for the initiates of my predecessors— those initiates or disciples of theirs who are still in this world and whom I can contact in the flesh. I also bring them into the fold so that they may know me and hear my voice. I will take them under my protection and help them also, and then there shall be one fold and one shepherd.

There is really no difference between the predecessor and his successor. Each Master merges in his own Master, his predecessor; and the disciples of the predecessor also merge in their Master, just as the disciples of the successor merge in their Master. So the Masters are one and their disciples are one, that is, all one fold.

> Therefore doth my Father love me, because I lay down my life, that I might take it again. *(10:17)*

---

1. "How think ye? if a man have an hundred sheep, and one of them be gone astray, doth he not leave the ninety and nine, and goeth into the mountains, and seeketh that which is gone astray?" *(Matt. 18:12)*.

He says: My Father loves me, because I do not hesitate to sacrifice anything in the interest of my disciples. Then, lest we think the Master will be *forced* to give his life, he explains:

> No man taketh it from me, but I lay it down of myself. I have power to lay it down, and I have power to take it again. This commandment have I received of my Father.   *(10:18)*

I am not bound by karmas in any way. I have taken this body only because my Father wanted me to come into this world. Others come into the world as a result of their sins, their own past actions. Those who are slaves of the mind and the senses are not free to come and go as they please, for they are bound within the domain of Kal, the negative power. Because my burden is light, I can help to pay the karmas of my disciples by taking some of them on myself.

I can leave this world whenever I want to, and I can come back into this world whenever I want to. I have come only because my Father wanted me to come, and I will leave only when my Father calls me back. "I lay down my life" means, I can leave the body whenever I wish; and "I take it again" means, I can also return whenever I wish. This commandment, this privilege, I have received from my Father.

> Then came the Jews round about him, and said unto him, How long dost thou make us to doubt? If thou be the Christ, tell us plainly.
> *(10:24)*

> Jesus answered them, I told you, and ye believed not: the works that I do in my Father's name, they bear witness of me.   *(10:25)*

> But ye believe not, because ye are not of my
> sheep, as I said unto you.   *(10:26)*

> My sheep hear my voice, and I know them, and
> they follow me.   *(10:27)*

Some people did not believe what he was saying. He
said: It is not your fault. Naturally you will not believe
me because you are not my sheep. You are not marked
for me. Those who are marked for me will automatically
be drawn to me. They will automatically have faith in
my teachings and follow them. So Sant Mat, the teachings of the Saints, is not for everybody.

> And I give unto them eternal life; and they shall
> never perish, neither shall any man pluck them
> out of my hand.   *(10:28)*

What will they get in reward for following me? They
will get eternal life, life from which they will never have
to come again to this world. At present we do not have
eternal life. Every time we take birth, then death starts
dancing before us, and we have to leave the body to take
birth again. "And they shall never perish." The whole
creation is perishable, but my disciples will never perish. They will escape from this perishable world.
"Neither shall any man pluck them out of my hand." He
says: Nobody can deprive me of my initiates. The seed
is planted. Even if they go astray, the seed will sprout
again. They will again come back to the path. They
cannot go elsewhere. They *must* go back to my Father's
house.

> My Father, which gave them me, is greater than
> all; and no man is able to pluck them out of my
> Father's hand.   *(10:29)*

I and my Father are one. *(10:30)*

Why can nobody deprive me of my allotted souls? Because my Father is the King of kings. Even Kal is not greater than my Father, because Kal has also been created by my Father. My Father is more powerful than anyone else in this whole creation, and I have become one with Him. He has given me all the power that He commands, so how can anybody deprive me of my marked souls?

Naturally the people never believed what he was saying, so they wanted to stone him.

> The Jews answered him, saying, For a good work we stone thee not; but for blasphemy; and because that thou, being a man, makest thyself God. *(10:33)*

We do not condemn you for doing good work. No doubt you are doing very good work, but we cannot tolerate that you, a man just like us, living like us, declare yourself God. That is why we want to stone you. Christ gives a very beautiful answer:

> . . . Is it not written in your law, I said, Ye are gods? *(10:34)*

He says: Find your own scriptures; you read the books written by Moses or the sermons given by John the Baptist. It is written very clearly in these scriptures that everyone is potentially God. What difference does it make if I have said that I am God? Even all of you are God—not only I. Every human being has the capacity to become God again. I have realized the Father, and you too can realize the Father. You are potentially God, but there is a covering over your soul. A diamond is a diamond, but it has lost its luster because it has been thrown into dirt. The diamond in the dirt has the same value as the diamond in the jeweler's shop, but we can get the full price for it only when we remove the dirt.

Some of you may believe in evolution, but the theory of evolution as taught today is only partially correct. In the beginning all souls came out of the Father, just as the drop comes out of the ocean. In the soul's descent into the world, it was given the mind, the body, and the senses as its servants, through which to function in this world. But now, instead of the soul dominating the servants, the servants and their deeds have become the ruler of the soul, and the soul is so hopelessly and helplessly bound and covered by countless layers of darkness and filth that it does not even know that the Father exists, much less that it is part of Him.

Man, in his present state, has degraded himself by indulging in sense pleasures and committing wicked deeds and atrocities that have placed him sometimes even below the status of an animal. Now that we are in the human body, we should take advantage of this golden opportunity by realizing the Father within ourselves.

> If he called them gods, unto whom the word of
> God came, and the scripture cannot be broken;
> *(10:35)*

> Say ye of him, whom the Father hath sanctified,
> and sent into the world, Thou blasphemest; be-
> cause I said, I am the Son of God?   *(10:36)*

We can become God only when we are attached to the Word of God by a living Master. All scriptures reveal this to us if we read them with understanding.

You cannot tolerate even my simple statement that I
am the Son of God, says Christ. But everyone is God,
because God is within every one of us. And those who
are attached to the Word of God can remove all the
coverings of filth and darkness from the soul and merge
back in God. Then they become God in reality. Others
are only potentially God.

> If I do not the works of my Father, believe me
> not.   *(10:37)*

> But if I do, though ye believe not me, believe the
> works: that ye may know, and believe, that the
> Father is in me, and I in him.   *(10:38)*

> And many resorted unto him, and said, John did
> no miracle: but all things that John spake of this
> man were true.   *(10:41)*

> And many believed on him there.   *(10.42)*

Then Jesus tells them that if he did not do the works
of his Father, he would not expect them to believe him.
But since he really does the works of his Father and they
still do not believe his words, they should at least believe the evidence of what they see. The essential thing
is that they should accept him as the Son of God, that
he is in the Father and the Father is in him. And many
did believe him and entered his fold. Their honest and
sincere efforts had marked them for the true fold, and
so they became "the chosen ones."

"The chosen people of God" does not refer only to
the Israelites, or Jews, but to all those who, under the
guidance of a living Master, are traveling on the path
back to Him, as designated by the Father himself. Being

a "chosen one" of the Lord has nothing to do with one's religion, sect, race, or nationality. Only they are chosen by the Lord who are sincere in their longing to return to the house of the Lord and who have love and devotion for Him and Him alone. That is to say, they are marked by Him to come on the path leading back to Him.

This is the path of the soul, but unless the mind is convinced that it too cannot be happy until it returns to its home, the second spiritual stage, it will not accompany the soul. And unless the mind accompanies the soul, and the soul is completely disentangled from it— which cannot happen until both reach the second stage—the soul is not free to go back to the Father. At present, the soul is a prisoner in this world and is attached to the mind and senses, which are constantly running down from the eye center. But when, under the guidance of a Master, we withdraw our attention to the eye center, and our soul, or consciousness, is concentrated there, then the mind and the soul can travel upward together.

At the same time, we should live a normal life and perform all our duties but should not become so entangled in worldly matters as to forget the real purpose of our being in this world. That purpose is to travel on the path leading to God-realization; and when we are on that path, we are in the fold of the good shepherd who will lead us home.

11

You all know the story of Lazarus and his sisters, Mary and Martha, who were close friends of Jesus. Lazarus was ill and his sisters sent for Jesus, but Lazarus died in the meantime. After two days, Jesus said to his disciples:

> . . . Our friend Lazarus sleepeth; but I go, that I
> may awake him out of sleep. *(11:11)*

We are all sleeping in this world, sleeping as far as our Lord is concerned. We are awake as far as the world is concerned. We are always conscious of this world, but we are not conscious of our real Source. The Master comes to awaken us from this slumber; he makes us realize that there is something much higher than the sensual pleasures. He also tells us how to attain perfect bliss, and guides us all the way back to the Father, but only if we have absolute faith in him. Otherwise we are easily deceived and may turn away from him at the crucial moment when we need his guidance most.

> . . . Thy brother shall rise again. *(11:23)*

We need never despair. No matter how far away from the Lord we may have strayed, if our attitude is right, if we have no ulterior motive whatsoever, the Lord himself will mark us for the path and put us in

touch with a living Master. The Master helps us to "rise
again" and takes us back to Him.

> I am the resurrection, and the life: he that be-
> lieveth in me, though he were dead, yet shall he
> live: *(11:25)*

> And whosoever liveth and believeth in me shall
> never die. Believest thou this?   *(11:26)*

Even though you may be dead as far as the Lord is
concerned, says Christ, if you have faith in me I will
resurrect you from this spiritual death and put you on
the path. When you are on the path, you are "living,"
and if you continue to have faith in me, you shall never
die. This does not mean that you will never die a physical death. It means that after you leave this physical
body, you will not have to come back to this world and
face death again. Nor will you again have to face this
spiritual death from which I have resurrected you to life
everlasting. You will never forget God, but will always
travel upwards on this path of Light and Sound until you
merge into Him and become God.

When Jesus or any living Master says "I," "me," or
"mine," he is not referring to himself as the physical
body, but to that Divine Power which sustains him: "I
and the Father are one" *(10:30).* The Father that dwells
in me does all things.[1]

At the command of Jesus, the stone was removed
from the cave in which the body of Lazarus had been
placed, and Jesus said to Martha:

---

1. ". . . I speak not of myself: but the Father that dwelleth in me, he doeth
the works" *(John 14:10).*

. . . Said I not unto thee, that, if thou wouldest
believe, thou shouldest see the glory of God?
(11:40)

Then they took away the stone from the place
where the dead was laid. And Jesus lifted up his
eyes, and said, Father, I thank thee that thou
hast heard me.   *(11:41)*

And I knew that thou hearest me always: but
because of the people which stand by I said it,
that they may believe that thou hast sent me.
(11:42)

Saints and the Father are one. The Saints have
reached that level of consciousness where language is
not necessary—the Father always hears them and they
always hear the Father. But for the sake of the people
around them who have not reached that level of consciousness, they sometimes do speak out loud to the
Father to enable the people to understand.

12

When a number of people began to follow Jesus, the chief priests and the Pharisees held consultations among themselves to put Jesus to death, because his popularity affected their income. Jesus was giving them spiritual teachings and charging them nothing, as no Saint accepts any remuneration for his teachings. Although Jesus was making a triumphant entry into Jerusalem, and the masses were honoring and praising him with great fanfare and waving of palms, he knew that he would be crucified within the week.

> . . . The hour is come, that the Son of man should be glorified. *(12:23)*

When Jesus said that he would be glorified, he was indicating that he would soon return to the Father and be one with Him. He knew that his end was approaching, as he had practically finished the allotted task assigned to him by the Father. Jesus therefore informs Philip and Andrew that he had glorified the Father while he was in the body by accomplishing the task given to him, and now he would be glorified by the Father as the Father would take him back to Himself.

> Verily, verily, I say unto you, Except a corn of wheat fall into the ground and die, it abideth alone: but if it die, it bringeth forth much fruit. *(12:24)*

Just as a seed cannot bring forth fruit unless it dies, we can never be spiritually fruitful and realize the Lord within ourselves until we have completely subdued our ego. As the seed has to merge in the earth in which it is planted, so has our ego to be eliminated, or be merged in the earth. If we do not get rid of our ego, we remain so full of our own vices that there is no room for the Lord, so we are "alone." We can never be conscious of the Lord as long as we are full of ego. As long as there is even one speck left in us, we are impure and not fit to bear the fruit of God-realization.

The opposite of ego is humility; the two cannot remain together. Ego will eventually leave us only when we develop the quality of humility within ourselves. And this humility must not be superficial—it must be real and true humility that comes naturally from within. Calculated and artificial humility is just like cosmetic jewelry. As long as we are attached to the objects and faces of this creation, we are full of ego, the very opposite of humility. Only attachment can create detachment in us. When we are attached to the Divine Melody within, we automatically become detached from this creation and are filled with genuine humility.

> He that loveth his life shall lose it; and he that hateth his life in this world shall keep it unto life eternal.   (12:25)

This means that one who has given himself to the sensual pleasures and is hankering after worldly possessions and achievements—and is thus attached to this creation—actually does not know what he is losing. By not making the best use of his life on this earth, he is losing the beautiful opportunity of attaining eternal life.

He has no idea of his great loss. But he who detaches himself from the worldly faces, possessions, and sensual pleasures will get that eternal life because he will go back to the Father and become the Father. He may have to suffer in this world to clear his fate karmas, or destiny, but his reward is great, for after leaving this world he will never have to face death again.

By hating one's life in this world, Christ did not mean that we should hate life; he meant we should hate the worldly type of life, we should detach ourselves from the sensual pleasures. In fact, we do not need to hate at all, for if we are absorbed in devotion to the Lord we are not even interested in the worldly life.

Some people may interpret this verse to mean that we should take our own life, but that would only add a greater sin to the already heavy load that we have accumulated throughout the ages. This human body was given to us by the Lord for the purpose of attaining God-realization, and if we destroy this precious gift—this vehicle that he has given us—we commit a great sin.

> If any man serve me, let him follow me; and where I am, there shall also my servant be: if any man serve me, him will my Father honour.
> *(12:26)*

When he said, "If any man serve me," Christ meant that if any man would live his teachings and serve him by doing the spiritual practice as instructed, he would automatically find the Radiant Form within himself. Christ says: As the Father and I are one, by serving me he serves the Father, and my Father will honor him by taking him back to Himself. And what greater honor can there be than to merge back into the Father!

Now is my soul troubled; and what shall I say?
Father, save me from this hour: but for this
cause came I unto this hour.   *(12:27)*

Jesus says: Now I feel perturbed—not for myself,
but for you, my disciples, whom I shall soon have to
leave. Until now you have had my external guidance,
but you can have it only as long as I am with you. What
should I say? How can I explain these things to you? I
know that my hour to leave this body has come and that
it is my Father's will that I should leave you. I am not at
all troubled on my own account. I am perfectly happy
and eager to return to my Father.

I only ask to be saved from my feelings for you, from
concern about what you will do without my physical
guidance when I am gone. There is a reason for my
leaving you like this. While I am with you in the flesh,
you are more or less complacent and depend just on my
physical guidance. But when I leave you, that longing to
be with me will automatically take you to my Radiant
Form within yourself. I will then merge you into myself
and take you to the Father, and we will both merge in
Him.

This proves how compassionate the Saints are and
how they look after their disciples with loving care.
Though they are not of this world and have come into
this world only by the will of the Father to redeem
certain souls allotted to them, they have great compassion for their devotees, especially those who have not
yet met their Radiant Form within. The Master knows
how miserable they will be, and yet this is the way it has
been ordained by the Father, for that very misery and
longing will actually drive them within to see their Master after he has left this world. While he is with them in

the flesh, they are content and happy to be with him physically and do not always make the necessary effort to meet him within. So after expressing his sympathy for them, Christ said, "but for this cause came I unto this hour."

> Father, glorify thy name. Then came there a
> voice from heaven, saying, I have both glorified
> it, and will glorify it again.   *(12:28)*

> The people therefore, that stood by, and heard
> it, said that it thundered: others said, An angel
> spake to him.   *(12:29)*

> Jesus answered and said, This voice came not
> because of me, but for your sakes.   *(12:30)*

Jesus asks the Father to glorify His name, and the Father replies: I have glorified my name through you, because you have put these people on the path. The Son is glorified because he has finished his allotted task, and the disciples marked by him are glorified because they have been put on the path.

Jesus prayed to the Father, not because he had to pray in order for the Father to hear him, but so that the disciples might also hear him praying to the Father and hear the Father glorifying Christ. The voice came from the Father in reply: I have glorified Jesus the Christ because he has finished his allotted task, he has put on the path the souls allotted to his care, and I will again glorify the souls he has put on the path, as marked by me, by pulling them to my own level.

> Now is the judgment of this world: now shall the
> prince of this world be cast out.   *(12:31)*

The prince of this world is Kal, the negative power, also known as Satan or Universal Mind, who looks after the whole creation. Everybody in this creation, whether he is Kal's devotee or not, lives in the domain of Kal. Christ says: When I sever my connections with my body, I automatically sever my connections with Kal, because it is only my body that lives within his domain. When I leave this body and go to my Father, I am in the highest region, which is far beyond the reach of Kal.

It is only the body that is bound by Kal's laws, and it will simply decay or be destroyed. Then the mind and soul, instead of taking another body, will each merge into their own source. The mind will merge in Universal Mind, and the soul will then be free to merge back in the Father in heaven.

I have nothing whatever to do with Satan, says Christ, but it was the Father's will that I live in Satan's domain and take certain souls out of his clutches. Now that those particular souls have come into my fold, I am leaving the domain of Kal, thus casting him out of my life.

> And I, if I be lifted up from the earth, will draw
> all men unto me.   *(12:32)*

Jesus again explains to his disciples why he is leaving them. He says, "If I be lifted up from the earth"; that is: When I go to my Father, I will draw with me all those whom I have initiated while I was in this world. Just as I will merge into the Father, my disciples will also be merged into the Father along with me. So I am happy to go, though I sympathize with your loneliness and sorrow, which you will have to endure until we meet within.

> Then Jesus said unto them, Yet a little while is
> the light with you. Walk while ye have light, lest
> darkness come upon you: for he that walketh in
> darkness knoweth not whither he goeth. *(12:35)*

Only a few days are left now that I will physically be with you. Do not think that I am going to guide the generations to come, thousands of years after me. I am in this world for only a little while. Ask for any guidance that you may need while I am still in the body. Those who have not contacted me within will miss my guiding Light, for after I leave this world, naturally I will not be able to contact you in the flesh. So do not let the darkness of ignorance overtake you, but get enlightenment while the Light of the world is still with you physically.

If you do not set foot on the path now while I am here to initiate you, but try to eliminate that darkness by yourself, you can never succeed. "He that walketh in darkness knoweth not whither he goeth." To live in the world without the living guidance is walking in the darkness.

What use should you make of my physical presence? Get initiation and lift up your consciousness to the eye center so that you can see that Light, that Radiant Form within you. That is the real guiding Light.

> While ye have light, believe in the light, that ye
> may be the children of light.   *(12:36)*

He says: While I can show you the Light, being at your level, believe in that Light—experience that Light through me. Christ himself is the Light, because he is the Word made flesh and there is Light and Divine

Melody in the Word. Just as a father loves his child, the Master also loves his disciples. So he says: Come to the level of that Light and become my child. Once you see that Light inside and merge in it, you become the children of Light. Then you get guidance outside in this world and also inside. Even if the Master leaves the body, the inner guidance is always there.

> Jesus cried and said, He that believeth on me, believeth not on me, but on him that sent me.
> *(12:44)*

The Masters are free from all ego and never refer to themselves personally, but always to the Father. So Jesus says: If you believe in me, you do not believe in this physical form but in the Father who sent me. If you love me, if you have faith in me and follow my teachings, then you love the Father who sent me, because the Father and I are one. I do not need your love and devotion, but I want you to go back to the Father, and that is His way of calling you back. Therefore if you love me and follow the teachings, actually you are loving the Father and are on your way back to Him.

> And he that seeth me seeth him that sent me.
> *(12:45)*

Whosoever will see my Radiant Form within himself is actually not seeing me but the One who sent me, because I and the Father are one. If you have not seen the Radiant Form of the Master within but have seen the living Master in the flesh, even then you will eventually go back to the Father. By seeing the physical form of the Master you will become attached to him, and that

attachment will enable you to see his Radiant Form
within. From that point you will travel upwards until
you merge in the Father. .

> I am come a light into the world, that whosoever
> believeth on me should not abide in darkness.
> *(12:46)*

This world is full of darkness and illusion. I have
come to give you the Light of understanding, the Light
of Truth. Have faith in me and follow my teachings, and
you will not have to come back in this world again and
again. You will be liberated from this darkness.

> And if any man hear my words, and believe not,
> I judge him not: for I came not to judge the
> world, but to save the world. *(12:47)*

Jesus, out of great compassion, patiently says: If
anyone hears my teachings and still does not believe, I
will not accuse him. I only pity him, because he does not
realize what he is missing. He does not know when he
will get the opportunity of even being in a human body
again, much less of coming in contact with a living
Master.

I have come into this world only to give advice and
guidance, and not to judge or condemn anybody. I simply want to help you to rise above your sins and weaknesses, to save you from your karmas, from birth and
death, and to take you back to the Father.

Saints come to save not the whole world but those
souls who follow the teachings. The Master comes to
save only them. Otherwise, "but to save the world"
means the whole world. They never come to save the

whole world, because as he has explained previously:
Only those people will believe in me whom my Father
wants to believe in me, who are my "marked sheep."
Only they will hear me and have faith in me. So Saints
do not come to save the whole world.

> He that rejecteth me, and receiveth not my
> words, hath one that judgeth him: the word that
> I have spoken, the same shall judge him in the
> last day.   *(12:48)*

> For I have not spoken of myself; but the Father
> which sent me, he gave me a commandment,
> what I should say, and what I should speak.
>   *(12:49)*

Here Christ says: My Father will judge those who
will not listen to my teachings. Whatever you may do in
this world, you will be judged by your own actions, your
own karmas. I do not judge you. I am only teaching what
the Father commanded me to teach. I am only obeying
His commandment.

> And I know that his commandment is life ever-
> lasting: whatsoever I speak therefore, even as
> the Father said unto me, so I speak.   *(12:50)*

If you follow the teachings, you will gain everlasting
life. All this comes to you direct from the Father. My
teachings are His teachings, and you must follow them
if you want to go back to Him.

13

We are told at the beginning of this chapter how Jesus washed his disciples' feet. This washing of the feet is a symbol of humility and meekness. Jesus wanted to show his disciples that if he, their Master, washed their feet, they should he willing to do the same for one another—in other words, that they should be humble and meek and helpful to one another on the path. All true Masters tell us that an advanced disciple never bosses over others; rather, the more advanced one is, the more humble and helpful he is to others without making a show of it.

The path is not an organization nor an organized religion. All the initiates belong equally to the fold of the one good shepherd and should be kind, understanding, and helpful to one another in the time of need. And by being helpful, Jesus simply means helping others to stand on their own legs, encouraging them by our own example to make the effort, for each one must make his own effort on the path.

> Then cometh he to Simon Peter: and Peter saith unto him, Lord, dost thou wash my feet? *(13:6)*

> Jesus answered and said unto him, What I do thou knowest not now; but thou shalt know hereafter.   *(13:7)*

Peter objected: How can we allow you, our Master, to wash our feet? As Peter was to be his successor, Jesus

said to him: You do not realize what I am doing now, but
you will later on. Because I am washing your feet, they
will learn to respect you as my successor and will cooperate with you. By washing the feet of all of you, I am
simply showing that I have equal love for all of you and
that you, as my successor, should also equally love all.

> . . . If I wash thee not, thou hast no part with
> me. *(13:8)*

This has a beautiful mystic meaning. Unless the
Master washes away our sins, we cannot merge in him
and cannot go back to the Father. But when we do the
spiritual practice according to his instructions, we clear
our karmas, we get rid of all our sins. The more sins we
have, the longer it takes, but ultimately we become pure
and merge in the Shabd, which is the real form of the
Master. Then we are part of him who has merged in the
Father.

> . . . He that is washed needeth not save to wash
> his feet, but is clean every whit: and ye are
> clean, but not all. *(13:10)*

The Master himself is "clean every whit" because he
has no karmas or sins of his own "save to wash his feet,"
which means all the karmas that he has taken on himself
for the benefit of his disciples and which he can easily
wash off when he sees fit to do so. "And ye [my dis-
ciples] are clean," says Christ, "but not all." Since you
are attached to the Word, you are in the process of being cleansed. In other words, you have been cleansed
to a certain extent by coming on the path, but you have
yet to make a lot of spiritual progress before you can

become absolutely pure and fit to merge in the Word, the Holy Ghost, the real form of the Master within you.

> Ye call me Master and Lord: and ye say well; for
> so I am.   *(13:13)*

He says: No doubt you address me as "Master," no doubt you address me as "Lord," and there is nothing wrong with it, because I am the Master, I am the Lord; but you have not washed yourself yet. You do not have as much faith in me as you should have.

> If I then, your Lord and Master, have washed
> your feet; ye also ought to wash one another's
> feet.   *(13:14)*

> For I have given you an example, that ye should
> do as I have done to you.   *(13:15)*

Christ is teaching his disciples to be humble. He says: I am your Master, and when you love me, you want to wash my feet. I have washed your feet to tell you that being the Lord, being the Master, I have washed the feet of the disciple, so the disciple should also wash the feet of other disciples. He means to say that when the Master loves us so much, we should also love one another. The Master is noble, pure, and we worldly people are dirty, yet he loves us; but we do not love our fellowmen, who are just like us. He says: When such a noble person loves even the dirty man, the dirty man should at least learn to love his brothers.

> Verily, verily, I say unto you, The servant is not
> greater than his lord; neither he that is sent
> greater than he that sent him.   *(13:16)*

The servant is never greater than the lord, and I, being the Lord, have washed your feet. So you, my disciple, should also try to behave in the same way with your own colleagues.

> If ye know these things, happy are ye if ye do them.   (13:17)

He says: You know these things intellectually, but you will be happy only when you practice them in your daily life.

> I speak not of you all: I know whom I have chosen: but that the scripture may be fulfilled. . . .   (13:18)

Christ says: I am appointing only one of you to succeed me as Master. It is mentioned in all the scriptures that a living Master is necessary to put those in touch with the Word who are ready and marked by the Father. Since I shall soon be leaving you, I am appointing a successor to look after you and to put new seekers on the path. He will look after those whom I have initiated and will also initiate the souls allotted to him by the Lord; so again there will be one shepherd and one fold, as ordained by the Father.

> . . . He that eateth bread with me hath lifted up his heel against me.   (13:18)

He is speaking about Judas. He says: I know he is to betray me. He has no faith in me, yet I love him. I do not tell people that he is going to betray me. I do not want to expose his sins. I still love him.

Now I tell you before it come, that, when it is come to pass, ye may believe that I am he.
(13:19)

Verily, verily, I say unto you, He that receiveth whomsoever I send receiveth me; and he that receiveth me receiveth him that sent me.
(13:20)

Again Christ is speaking to them about his successor. He says: Now while I am in the flesh I am trying to guide you and to tell you that soon I shall be leaving you. I also want you to know that I am appointing a successor and that there is no difference between him and me. For you, I am in my successor and my successor is in me. And for those whom he initiates, he is in the Father and the Father is in him. It all amounts to the same thing, for we are all one. All realized souls are one in the Father and the Father is in them.

Whoever recognizes as my successor that person whom I shall appoint to carry on the teachings, will actually be showing love and faith in me, because it is my wish that you look upon me as your Master *while I am in the flesh*. Since I and the Father are one, you will also be honoring the Father by loving and respecting the one whom I shall select to guide you.

Now Jesus is trying to tell his disciples that his end is very near. He says:

. . . Now is the Son of man glorified, and God is glorified in him. *(13:31)*

My allotted time and work in this world is almost finished; and as soon as it is, I will be glorified in my Father because I shall go back to Him. And my Father is glorified in me because I have done only what He wanted me to do.

> If God be glorified in him, God shall also glorify
> him in himself, and shall straightway glorify
> him.   *(13:32)*

Christ again says: There is no difference between
me and God. If I am glorified in God, God is also glorified in me. I am happy that I have been able to do my
duty. Whatever had been assigned to me by my Father,
that I have done.

> Little children, yet a little while I am with you.
> Ye shall seek me: and as I said unto the Jews,
> Whither I go, ye cannot come; so now I say to
> you.   *(13:33)*

The "little children" are the new initiates, those who
have just come into the fold. They are like little children
because they will need further guidance after the departure of their Master. They have not yet learned to walk
on the path and still need the Master's guiding hand. As
a mother gives more attention to the little child, so the
Master gives greater attention to the new disciples.
You will seek me, but where I am you cannot come,
Christ says, because you have not yet reached that
spiritual height; so I am telling you now that after I am
gone, you should follow the one whom I have chosen to
succeed me. I am only going to leave you physically; my
Radiant Form will still be with you. But the physical
guidance which you are getting from me now, you will
continue to get from my successor. You cannot yet see
my Radiant Form within yourself, but when you are
sufficiently advanced or are absolutely pure, then you
will join me and merge in the Father. Until then, go to
my successor for the spiritual advice that you need from
the physical form of the Master.

> A new commandment I give unto you, That ye
> love one another; as I have loved you, that ye
> also love one another.   *(13:34)*

Here Christ emphasizes to the new initiates that they should try to strengthen one another's faith by loving one another. The Master loves his disciples, so when they love one another that means they are loving their Master. They see their own Master in every disciple. Actually, they love one another because they love the Master. For them he is the center around which everything revolves. When disciples meet with this attitude, their love for the Master will grow and their love for one another will grow.

This does not refer to the personal or physical attraction that people mistakenly call love. Anything that takes the attention below the eye center is not spiritual love, but a mere deception, a trick of the mind and senses and an excuse for our own weaknesses. A person who has spiritual love, loves everybody and not just a few people.

> By this shall all men know that ye are my disci-
> ples, if ye have love one to another.   *(13:35)*

You should be a living example of your Master's teachings. That will be more convincing proof that you are my disciples than any professing.

> . . . Whither I go, thou canst not follow me
> now; but thou shalt follow me afterwards.
>   *(13:36)*

Just because you are not able to follow me now does not mean that you will never be able to come where I am going. You will definitely reach that inner stage, but it will take some time because you have yet a lot of karmas to pay off in this world, a lot of sins to be washed. But when the layers of darkness that cover the soul have been removed by devotion to the Word, then nothing can prevent the soul from merging back in the Father, to whom I am going. So in the meantime, try to love one another.

> Peter said unto him, Lord, why cannot I follow thee now? I will lay down my life for thy sake.
> *(13:37)*

> Jesus answered him, Wilt thou lay down thy life for my sake? Verily, verily, I say unto thee, The cock shall not crow, till thou hast denied me thrice. *(13:38)*

The Master always knows where we stand in our faith and love, but sometimes we have the misconception that we love the Master very much and have implicit faith in him. He does not have to put us to the test to know where we stand, but sometimes he tests us to make us realize how shallow our love and faith actually are.

When Peter said to Christ, I would like to follow you now, I will lay down my life for your sake, Jesus wanted to make him realize where he stood in his faith and love. Therefore Jesus answered: You say you will lay down your life for my sake, but I say to you, the cock shall not crow till you have denied me thrice. Of course, Peter could not believe that he would ever do such a thing, but after he actually did deny Christ three times and heard the cock crow, he realized that his love and faith were superficial.

14

Let not your heart be troubled: ye believe in
God, believe also in me. *(14:1)*

Christ says: Do not feel troubled—just as a father
who goes out of his house for a long journey tries to
console his children by telling them, "I will bring pres-
ents for you," or "I will call you there very soon; just
love one another, try to live happily in this house."
Christ was only physically leaving his disciples, both
old and new, and he was trying to console them.

In my Father's house are many mansions: if it
were not so, I would have told you. I go to prepare a place for you. *(14:2)*

There are many spiritual stages on the way, right
from the eye center up to the end of the journey. We
have to go through many stages, or "mansions," and
everyone gets a place in them according to his spiritual
attainment. Christ does not say that everyone will go
straight to the Father. We may get release from this
flesh, but there is still a long way to go back to the Lord.
Every disciple does not go straight to the Father. How
far he goes depends upon his own spiritual progress; he
may reach the first, second, third, fourth, or fifth stage.
So every person has his own place, prepared for him by
his Master, and continues to make progress from there
onward until he finally merges into the Father.

So Christ is saying to his disciples: Now I am going to prepare the place that you will reach during this lifetime, and at the time of your death I will receive you and place you in one of the mansions of my Father's house.

> And if I go and prepare a place for you, I will come again, and receive you unto myself; that where I am, there ye may be also.   *(14:3)*

Do not think that you, by yourself, will have to find the place which I will prepare for you. "I will come again and receive you unto myself"—"again" means: I will come at the time of your death in my Radiant Form. You will merge into my Radiant Form. Then I will take you to a mansion in my Father's house according to your own spiritual progress, and from there you will work your way upward until you return to the Father. So do not be concerned at all, because where I am, there you also will be, provided you have faith in me and turn to me at the time of your death.

> And whither I go ye know, and the way ye know.
> *(14:4)*

You know where I am going, for I have told you that I am going back to my Father. And you also know the way, because I have initiated you and put you on the path so that you may also reach the place where I am going. Continue on that path. The road, the path, leads *straight* back to the Father. If you keep straight on that path, *automatically* you will find me within yourself.

> . . . I am the way, the truth and the life:

no man cometh unto the Father, but by me.
(14:6)

The real form of the Master is not the physical body, but the Word. Actually, the Word is our Master. The physical body of the living Saint is our Master, because the Word has taken abode in that flesh. He is "the Word made flesh." The disciple is not the body nor is the Master the body. The soul is the disciple and the Word is the Master.

What Jesus means here is that the Word, or Shabd, is the way, the truth, and the life. It is the way, because through the Word we find our way back to the Father. It is the truth, because it never perishes. It has created the whole universe. Everything we see will perish, but not that Creative Power, the Word. It is the life, because the Word gives us eternal life.

This path has been the same from the very beginning, and will always be the same. Christ said in a previous chapter: These teachings are not mine—they come from my Father. The teachings have been the same ever since man was created; and you can know this truth only through me, the living Master, by getting initiated and following the path according to my instructions. Nobody can reach the Father direct. You have to be accepted by a perfect living Master and follow the path. Then, stage by stage, mansion by mansion, you will reach the ultimate destination.

If ye had known me, ye should have known my Father also: and from henceforth ye know him, and have seen him. *(14:7)*

This is something very beautiful. You have seen me, Christ says, and if you have faith in me and love me, then you have also seen the Father, for the Father is in me and I am in the Father. The physical body is only a covering over the mind and soul, which enables them to function together in this world. I have come from the Father direct and I will merge back in Him as soon as I leave this physical body. And when you leave your physical body, you will merge in my Radiant Form, provided you have followed the path as instructed. After I have taken you through the mansions of my Father's house according to the spiritual progress you have made, you will also eventually merge in the Father.

This consolation is directed mainly at the new initiates, those who have just come on the path and have not yet made much progress. We are *always* making progress no matter how feeble our meditation seems to be, but the soul has such a huge mountain of darkness to bore through that no matter how far it has gone, until it sees some Light it feels that it has made no progress at all. There is nothing by which to gauge one's progress within until we see some Light, but His grace is always there; and with faith, devotion, and effort, we continue to make progress whether we are aware of it or not. But once we have seen some Light and heard at least the echo of the Celestial Music, the way is easy and we become happier as we go along.

When we have advanced to the stage where we meet the Radiant Form of the Master and merge in him, then there is absolutely no room for doubt nor any danger of our straying from the path; we will go quickly from there to our eternal home of perfect and everlasting peace and bliss.

Philip saith unto him, Lord, shew us the Father, and it sufficeth us.   *(14:8)*

Philip says: We believe you and we know that if we have seen you, we have seen the Father, but why do you not show us the Father? Jesus replies:

> Have I been so long time with you, and yet hast thou not known me, Philip? he that hath seen me hath seen the Father; and how sayest thou then, Shew us the Father?   *(14:9)*

Earlier Christ has said that God came down to the level of a human being when He came to this world in the form of a Master—"He was in the world, and the world was made by Him, and the world knew Him not." You have seen me, says Jesus, and I have been with you for a long time. What greater proof do you want that I am in the Father and the Father is in me? If you do not have even this much faith in me, then how can you expect to go back to the Father?

> Believest thou not that I am in the Father, and the Father in me? the words that I speak unto you I speak not of myself: but the Father that dwelleth in me, he doeth the works. *(14:10)*

There is no difference between me and my Father. You are spiritually blind and deaf, you cannot see and hear Him in the Spirit. Therefore, out of His mercy and grace He has come down to your level in the physical form to instruct you and put you on the path leading back to Him. It is He that you see in the physical form and it is He who is teaching you. I do nothing. It is the Father who is doing everything.

> Believe me that I am in the Father and the Father in me: or else believe me for the very works' sake.   *(14:11)*

Jesus then says: If you cannot believe that there is no difference between me and the Father, at least believe in me because of my works. You know that no ordinary human being could do this work that the Father in me is doing. If you do not believe me, then at least judge from the work that is being done by the Father.

> Verily, verily, I say unto you, He that believeth
> on me, the works that I do shall he do also; and
> greater works than these shall he do; because I
> go unto my Father.   *(14:12)*

The Master is always steeped in Shabd, the Word, so he is always creating love and devotion for the Word in us. Therefore, says Christ, if you have faith in me, you will love me and will also be able to do what I am doing.

Christ is referring to his successor when he says: Greater works than these shall he do, because I go to my Father. Every Master always praises his successor and says that the successor will be greater than he is. You will remember that John the Baptist also said the same about Christ. They do this out of great humility and to inspire faith and confidence in their disciples for the successor. Otherwise, the disciple might think that the successor is only one of us—he is our brother disciple, how can he all of a sudden be the living Master?

When the Master appoints a successor, it is the Father who is doing so through him, and the Father also makes the successor fit to be a perfect Master, for then the Father is in him and he is in the Father, like any other perfect Master. If the disciples really love their own Master, they will have faith in the successor appointed by him, and will also love him. They will realize that it is the Father who is incarnated in the flesh of the successor, just as He was in their own Master; that it is the Father who is doing the work, just as He did through their own Master. All Masters are great, but the predecessor always claims that his successor will be greater.

> And whatsoever ye shall ask in my name, that
> will I do, that the Father may be glorified in the
> Son.   *(14:13)*

> If ye shall ask any thing in my name, I will do it.
>   *(14:14)*

He says: Whatever you will ask me in my love, in my name, will be granted. All your wishes will be fulfilled, because I am in the Father and I am the owner of all that the Father has. If you ask me for something from the treasure of the Father, that whole treasure has been entrusted to me, so I will give you whatever you want from that treasure. You have to approach the Father through me. He does not hear directly at all. So if you want the Father to hear your prayer, you must pray to your Master within.

> If ye love me, keep my commandments. *(14:15)*

Then he says: Do not forget one thing—always live up to the teachings, always remain on the path and attached to the Word. And what is Christ's commandment? Love one another. You should be so much in love with the Master that you see nothing but the Master in whomsoever you meet. That is the only way you can really love one another. Otherwise it is impossible.

> And I will pray the Father, and he shall give you
> another Comforter, that he may abide with you
> for ever;   *(14:16)*

> Even the Spirit of truth; whom the world cannot
> receive, because it seeth him not, neither know-
> eth him: but ye know him; for he dwelleth with
> you, and shall be in you.   *(14:17)*

I will ask my Father to shower upon you the grace of
the Holy Ghost, or Word. That is the only thing which
can give you comfort in this world. God and the Word
are the same, and just as the Father never dies, so the
Shabd, or Word, also abides forever. Thus, when you
are in contact with that Word you are in contact with the
Father.

Worldly people cannot receive the Spirit of Truth—
the Shabd—because that Spirit cannot be seen with the
physical eyes, and the worldly people are slaves of the
senses. But you know that Spirit; you have been attached to it at the time of initiation. It dwells within you,
and it will always be there to guide you.

Why is the Holy Ghost known as the Comforter?
Because when we are attached to the Holy Ghost within, we are at peace and we experience happiness, bliss,
and comfort. Now we are all at war within ourselves.
When we are attached to that Spirit within, we are
contented, we are at peace within ourselves. So he says:
I will always be in touch with you through that Comforter. I will always be sending you the Comforter—
the Sound from within—in greater abundance, so you
should therefore continue to hear that Spirit.

> I will not leave you comfortless: I will come to
> you.   *(14:18)*

You will never be orphaned, Christ tells his disciples. I will always be with you to comfort and guide you

if you turn to me for guidance. I am always ready to help
you.

> Yet a little while, and the world seeth me no
> more; but ye see me: because I live, ye shall live
> also.   *(14:19)*

It is very beautiful. He says: The world will not see
me when I leave this body, but you will still see me
because I am not going to leave you. Where will you see
me? Within yourself. I will always be with you in my
Radiant Form, so for you I do not die. "Because I live,
ye shall live also." I live forever. I cannot die. When you
see me inside, you will also never die. The Master never
leaves, he never dies. He is always with the disciple.
Even though the Master is no longer at our level, the
disciple can still go up to the Master's level when he has
made sufficient progress on the path.

The Master within is continually attracting the disciple upward, and the purer the soul, the sooner it
contacts the inner Master, the Word. As long as we are
caught by the attachments and pleasures of this world,
we are not even aware of that attraction. But when we
do the spiritual practice as instructed, we are gradually
cleansed of our sins and become pure and receptive to
his grace. It is his grace—in other words, the Shabd, or
Holy Ghost—that draws us up to his Radiant Form, so
that we may live in him and he in us.

> At that day ye shall know that I am in my Father,
> and ye in me, and I in you.   *(14:20)*

He says: Now I am in the flesh, so you do not realize
that the Father and I are one. I am just like you in this

body. But when you see me inside, you will have no doubt left. Then you will know that what I am saying is true. The real form of the disciple is the Spirit; the real form of the Master is also the Spirit, and that Spirit comes from the Father and merges back in the Father. So we will all become the Father.

> He that hath my commandments, and keepeth
> them, he it is that loveth me: and he that loveth
> me shall be loved of my Father, and I will love
> him, and will manifest myself to him. (14:21)

Every one of you says that he loves me, every one of you is showing devotion to me, but who is my real lover? He who keepeth my commandment—who lives in my teachings, who has changed the pattern of his life, who is attending to the Word, or Spirit within. Merely saying "I love you" is meaningless. If you really love me, you will keep my teachings in your heart twenty-four hours a day.

"And he that loveth me shall be loved of my Father." And one who has detached himself from the whole world and has attached himself to me, actually has attached himself to the Father. He has not fallen in love with me but with the Father. "And I will love him and will manifest myself to him." He says: I will also love him and show him my Radiant Form according to his longing and receptivity.

> . . . If a man love me, he will keep my words:
> and my Father will love him, and we will come
> unto him, and make our abode with him. (14:23)

Christ has just said, I will manifest myself to each disciple. Now he says, "We will come unto him, and make our abode with him." Those of you who love me will follow my instructions. "And my Father will love him" because my Father loves only those who are always in touch with the Spirit within. Then you will become clean and pure and will be fit to merge into the Father. And as the Father has merged into me and I into Him, we will abide within you and eventually we will all become one.

This is what is meant by the Holy Trinity—the Father, the Son, and the Holy Ghost. The real form of the Master, the Son of God, is the Word, or Spirit. The Word emanates from the Father and goes back to the Father, so the Lord, the Master, and the Word are three in one, or the Holy Trinity.

But we cannot understand this truth unless we experience it, and we can experience it only when we free the soul from the domination of the mind and senses through the practice of the Word as taught by the Master. When the soul becomes free from mind and senses, that is self-realization; and only through self-realization can we attain God-realization and merge back into the Father.

> He that loveth me not keepeth not my sayings:
> and the word which ye hear is not mine, but the
> Father's which sent me. *(14:24)*

Those who do not love me have actually no love for the Father. They will not accept the teachings; they will not attach themselves to the Word. But the teachings that I give you are not mine, nor is the Word that you have received from me at the time of initiation. Nothing belongs to me. It all comes from the Father who sent me. You are, in fact, attached to the Father when you are attached to the Word. If you really love me, you will follow my teachings and attach yourself to the Word, the Spirit within yourself.

> These things have I spoken unto you, being yet
> present with you.   *(14:25)*

How does the Master help us while he is in the flesh? He helps us to understand the teachings so that we will want to put them into practice and prove these truths to ourselves. He helps us from without as well as from within, but he can help us from without only as long as he is present in the physical form. He is continually guiding us from within, but we are not aware of it until we meet his Radiant Form inside, which we can do only by following the instructions he gives us while he is in the human body.

> But the Comforter, which is the Holy Ghost,
> whom the Father will send in my name, he shall
> teach you all things, and bring all things to your
> remembrance, whatsoever I have said unto
> you.   *(14:26)*

Jesus says: Do not worry that you will be lost after I leave. If you do the spiritual practice with love and devotion, then the Comforter, which is my real form, will always keep you in my love, and will keep you on the path while you are in this physical world. As long as you are sincere in your attitude, you will not go astray. And after you merge in my Radiant Form within yourself, you will have no doubts or questions. You will be above the reach of the mind and senses, which have a tendency to pull you down. You will be merged into that brilliant Light and sweet Sound, my Radiant Form, which will guide and protect you all the way. Then you will remember what I am telling you now, while in the flesh.

The Shabd, or Sound Current, is also referred to as the Holy Ghost. In the third chapter Christ says, "The wind bloweth where it listeth, and thou hearest the sound thereof, but canst not tell whence it cometh and whither it goeth." The Sound is invisible to the physical eyes, and therefore it is called a Ghost. The doors and windows may be closed and still a ghost can come in, and one does not know from where, how, or when it enters. The Shabd manifests itself to us in the same way within, at the eye center. Hence it is also called a Ghost. But since the word *ghost* normally denotes the soul of a dead person, a disembodied spirit that haunts living persons, the Shabd is referred to as the Holy Ghost. It is definitely not the soul of a dead person; it is the Sound, or Word of God, and it is holy because it comes from the Father and takes us back to the Father. So Christ refers to It as the Holy Ghost.

> Peace I leave with you, my peace I give unto
> you: not as the world giveth, give I unto you.
> Let not your heart be troubled, neither let it be
> afraid.   (14:27)

That peace I speak of cannot be found in this world, because here there is nothing but strife, struggle, and conflict. Lasting peace can never be found within the domain of the mind and senses. So it was from the time of creation, and so will it always be. We can get peace only when we return to our destination, our home. One who is away from his home, away from his land, can never find peace. Christ says: The real peace, which is of the Father, I have within myself because I am attached to the Holy Ghost, and that peace I give to you by attaching you to the Holy Ghost. As you follow my instructions, you too will radiate that peace from within yourselves.

Neither Christ nor any other Master has ever come to bring peace in this world. They come to bring heavenly peace to the souls allotted to them by the Father. Christ tells his disciples: Let not your heart be troubled or afraid. You will attain that everlasting peace, that wonderful bliss that is beyond the comprehension of the mind and intellect.

> Ye have heard how I said unto you, I go away, and come again unto you. If ye loved me, ye would rejoice, because I said, I go unto the Father: for my Father is greater than I. (14:28)

Naturally the disciples were confused, because Christ says that he is going to leave them as far as the physical body is concerned but that he will come again unto them. How can a man come inside another man? At that time the new initiates, his little children, though they were grown men, did not understand that Christ was leaving only his physical body, but that later on, as they advanced on the path according to the instructions he had given them, they would see him in his Radiant Form within themselves. That is how he would come again, within them.

Christ says: You should be happy that I am going back to my Father, for I am not of this world and this world is not my home. I am here only because my Father sent me down to this level to do His work. Now that my task in this world is finished, I am happy to go back to my Father in heaven, my true home. If you were sent down into some dark and filthy dungeon to do some work, you would perform your duty, but when that duty is finished, how happy you would be to go up again into fresh air and bright daylight.

This whole world, comparatively speaking, is a dark and filthy dungeon into which the Father has sent me to take you out of it and bring you back to Him. Therefore, if you love me, you will also rejoice that my task here is finished and that I am going back to the Father, especially since I will also draw you out of this dark dungeon, back to the Father, as soon as you have been cleansed of all your karmas or sins.

The love and devotion that the Master creates in us by his physical presence ultimately leads us back to him and thus to the Father.

> And now I have told you before it come to pass,
> that, when it is come to pass, ye might believe.
> *(14:29)*

Jesus says: I have told you all these things now, while I am still in the flesh, because you are not sufficiently advanced to be able to hear or see me inside, so I cannot explain these things to you within. I am therefore explaining everything to you now so that when I leave this world you may not feel perturbed in separation and troubled that I am not with you.

> Hereafter I will not talk much with you: for the
> prince of this world cometh, and hath nothing
> in me. *(14:30)*

The whole creation, including the material out of which the human body is made, belongs to Kal, or

Satan—the prince of this world, the negative power—so my body will go back to him at the time of my death. He is coming for this body of mine and I shall give it back to him, but he is no part of my real self and I shall immediately leave his domain as soon as I have shed the body. I have only a little time left with you because I am soon going to leave the flesh.

> But that the world may know that I love the Father; and as the Father gave me commandment, even so I do. Arise, let us go hence.
> *(14:31)*

The world should know that I love the Father, for I have given the teachings as commanded by Him. I have performed the task He commanded me to do. I have explained all these things to you before I leave this world so that you may believe and follow the commandment of my Father, and thus be saved and enjoy everlasting life. "Arise"—that is: Take your consciousness, your attention, up to the eye center. And "go hence," which means: Leave this dark den of iniquity and attain that eternal light, peace, and bliss.

15

I am the true vine, and my Father is the hus-
bandman.   *(15:1)*

Every branch in me that beareth not fruit he
taketh away: and every branch that beareth
fruit, he purgeth it, that it may bring forth more
fruit.   *(15:2)*

Those who come to me, they alone will be able to go
back to the Father. Those who do not have faith in me
are just like dry and withered branches that will be cut
off; they will have to come back into this world again.
Those who have faith in me bear the fruit of spiritual
progress. They will be purged of their sins so that they
may make still more progress. The more effort we
make, the more grace we receive to make still more
effort until we reach our goal. Then he says:

Now ye are clean through the word which I
have spoken unto you.   *(15:3)*

You have become clean and pure by attaching yourselves to the Word, the Holy Ghost, or Shabd, that you
received from me at the time of initiation.

Abide in me, and I in you. As the branch cannot
bear fruit of itself, except it abide in the vine; no
more can ye, except ye abide in me.   *(15:4)*

Through the Word, you abide in me and I in you. Just as a branch is barren of fruit without the main vine or trunk, so you cannot attain everlasting life unless you merge in my Radiant Form. When you abide in me, then your efforts will bear fruit.

> I am the vine, ye are the branches: He that abideth in me, and I in him, the same bringeth forth much fruit; for without me ye can do nothing.   (15:5)

Here Christ emphasizes what he has just told them: unless we merge in the Master within ourselves, and the Master in his Shabd Form merges in us, we can never bear fruit, we can make no spiritual progress. Unless we are attached to the Shabd, or Word, everything that we do—good as well as bad—is within the scope of the mind and senses, and our already heavy load of sins, or karmas, thus increases. When according to the instructions of the Master we raise our consciousness to the eye center and submit ourselves to the will of the Master, we merge in his Radiant Form and he merges in us. But without the help of the living Master we can do nothing.

> If a man abide not in me, he is cast forth as a branch, and is withered; and men gather them, and cast them into the fire, and they are burned.   (15:6)

Christ is saying here that the people who do not seek and gain the shelter of the living Master, but try to find God by themselves, are deceived by the negative power into thinking that they are on the right path. They cannot avoid becoming victims of the senses and worldly possessions, so spiritually they die and become like withered branches that are gathered, cast into the fire, and burned. This means that despite all their efforts they accomplish nothing spiritually, but only bind themselves even more tightly to this world, into which they have to be born again and again. Even then they are not sure that they will get a human birth. They may have to incarnate in many lower species of life before they are again entitled to a human body.

Christ and all other perfect Masters urge us to make the best use of the human body while we have it, and make real spiritual progress. For once we are on the path under the guidance of a Master, we need never come back in this world unless we have unfulfilled desires that bring us back. Even then, we never have to come back into a species of life lower than that of a human being, and we shall always have a better birth from the spiritual point of view—improved circumstances for making spiritual progress. But the beautiful part is that we need not come back in this world at all unless we are attached to it.

> If ye abide in me, and my words abide in you, ye
> shall ask what ye will, and it shall be done unto
> you.   *(15:7)*

When we have contact with that Shabd, that Light and Sound which is the Radiant Form of the Master, then whatever we ask the Master within will be given to us. And what do we ask from the Father once we are attached to the Shabd? We ask only for the Father from the Father, and then we are successful in our meditation, then we go back to the Father.

> Herein is my Father glorified, that ye bear much
> fruit; so shall ye be my disciples.   *(15:8)*

My Father is glorified because you have become
clean and pure, because you have made spiritual progress, or borne fruit, by being attached to the Shabd, or
Nam. By following my instructions, you have really
become my disciples in Truth and in Spirit.

> As the Father hath loved me, so have I loved
> you: continue ye in my love.   *(15:9)*

As the Father loves me, so I also love you, says
Christ. I am going to leave you only as far as my phys-
ical body is concerned; so continue the spiritual prac-
tice, the practice of Shabd to which I have attached you.
That is the real way of expressing your love for the
Father and for me.

> If ye keep my commandments, ye shall abide in
> my love; even as I have kept my Father's com-
> mandments, and abide in his love.   *(15:10)*

He says: Keeping my commandments, living the
teachings, is abiding in me, loving me. If you are not
following my instructions, it is absolute self-deception
to say that you love the Master.

> These things have I spoken unto you, that my
> joy might remain in you, and that your joy might
> be full.   *(15:11)*

I have tried to explain all these things to you so that
when I leave this world you may be happy in the knowledge that I have merged back in the Father and that you

also will merge in me, so that we will both be with the Father. Meanwhile, I am always with you in my Radiant Form, so you should be happy knowing that I am happy and that you will also reach that state of perfect bliss.

> This is my commandment, That ye love one
> another, as I have loved you.   (15:12)

When I am gone from this world, do not forget this fundamental principle of the teachings of all Saints: love one another.

> Greater love hath no man than this, that a man
> lay down his life for his friends.   (15:13)

When we make progress on the path according to the instructions of the Master, we are no longer slaves and servants of the mind and the senses. He brings us up to his level; we become his friends, his brothers. The Master has come into the world just for this purpose. He has come down to our level and laid down his life for us. No love could be greater, for even to come down to the level of a human being he has to take on some karmas to get a human body. He lays down his life of perfect bliss with the Father in order to come into the dark and filthy dungeon of this world; he tells us how to get out of it; he puts us on the path and even carries some of our load himself, just to bring us up to his level of supreme and eternal happiness.

> Ye are my friends, if ye do whatsoever I com-
> mand you.   (15:14)

We always try to please our friends and try to live in their wishes. Christ says: What greater friendship can there be than that you live in my teachings so that you may escape from the prison of this world! Then he says:

> Henceforth I call you not servants; for the ser-
> vant knoweth not what his lord doeth: but I have
> called you friends; for all things that I have
> heard of my Father I have made known unto
> you.   *(15:15)*

Up until now I have been calling you servants, because a servant or an employee does not know the will of his master or employer. He simply has to do what he is told to do and has no right to question the orders given to him. But now that you have followed my instructions, have been attached to the Word and have made sufficient progress to merge in me, you are my equals and I call you friends. As a friend, I have also shared with you all the things that my Father has told me. As servants, you knew neither me nor my Father, but through your faith in me you have become my equal and will also know the Father. Not only have we become friends, but we have merged and become one.

> Ye have not chosen me, but I have chosen you,
> and ordained you, that ye should go and bring
> forth fruit, and that your fruit should remain:
> that whatsoever ye shall ask of the Father in my
> name, he may give it you.   *(15:16)*

Do not think that you have selected me as your Master; I have chosen you. I have called you and have drawn you near me. It was in your destiny. It was so ordained by my Father. It was also decreed by my Father that you should bear fruit, that you should make spiritual progress. He selected you and has called you to

Him through me. And as the Father will do whatever I ask Him, He will also give you whatever you ask of Him in my name.

> These things I command you, that ye love one
> another.   *(15:17)*

I again want to impress upon you, Christ says, that you must all love one another.

> If the world hate you, ye know that it hated me
> before it hated you.   *(15:18)*

Christ tells his followers: Do not worry about public opinion and the criticism you get from worldly people for following the path. When the world has always hated me, why should you think it will spare you? Every lover of the Lord has to face criticism and sometimes even persecution at the hands of the world. But you do not belong to the world; you belong to the Father. Worldly people love only those who are attached to the world, so it is a folly to expect them to love you.

> If ye were of the world, the world would love his
> own: but because ye are not of the world, but I
> have chosen you out of the world, therefore the
> world hateth you.   *(15:19)*

You do not belong to this world. By the grace of the Father I have chosen to take you out of this world, so naturally the worldly people hate you.

> Remember the word that I said unto you, The
> servant is not greater than his lord. If they have
> persecuted me, they will also persecute you; if

they have kept my saying, they will keep yours
also.   (15:20)

When the people of the world have persecuted the
Saints, the lovers of the Lord, and they are also per-
secuting me, how can you expect better treatment from
them? So you also may have to suffer. But do not lose
your balance or feel perturbed. Keep your faith firm and
your attention in the Word—your Master within—and
you will rise above this domain of the mind and senses.

But all these things will they do unto you for my
name's sake, because they know not him that
sent me.   (15:21)

Jesus says: Because these people know nothing
about the Father and have no devotion, they do not
know Him who sent me to choose you. So they will
persecute you because you have faith in me. But I again
repeat: remain staunch in your faith, and their taunts
will not affect you.

If I had not come and spoken unto them, they
had not had sin: but now they have no cloke for
their sin.   (15:22)

If I had not told them that my Father has sent me,
they would have been able to plead ignorance, and
being ignorant they would not have committed a sin by
hating me, because they would not have known who I
am. But now they cannot plead ignorance. They have no
cloak, no excuse, because I have made it clear that I am
the Son of God.

> He that hateth me hateth my Father also.
> *(15:23)*

Those who have not seen the Father in me, and hate me, hate my Father also.

> If I had not done among them the works which none other man did, they had not had sin: but now they have both seen and hated both me and my Father. *(15:24)*

If I had not remained in God's will, if I had not performed the task in the world as allotted to me by my Father, they would have had an excuse. But they have seen the works that the Father has done through me, and they have also seen the Father because they have seen me, so now they have no excuse for their sin.

> But this cometh to pass, that the word might be fulfilled that is written in their law, They hated me without a cause. *(15:25)*

He says: In every age whenever Mystics come, people hate them. Every scripture says this.

> But when the Comforter is come, whom I will send unto you from the Father, even the Spirit of truth, which proceedeth from the Father, he shall testify of me: *(15:26)*

When the Comforter, the Holy Ghost, whom I shall send to you from the Father, is manifested to you, then you will have peace and contentment, Christ reassures his disciples. When you are attached to the Holy Ghost—the Shabd, or Nam—then you will be firm in your faith and will not in the least be concerned about public opinion.

> And ye also shall bear witness, because ye have
> been with me from the beginning. *(15:27)*

"From the beginning" means from the time of initiation, not from the time of creation. Since you have been with me from the time of your initiation, Christ says, you can also testify that I have clearly explained to these people that I am the Son of God and that I am doing the works of my Father. They cannot plead ignorance, and therefore have no excuse whatsoever for hating me and my Father.

16

> These things have I spoken unto you, that ye
> should not be offended.   *(16:1)*

I have told you these things to prepare you, so that when they take place you may not be taken unawares, be hurt, and lose faith.

> They shall put you out of the synagogues: yea,
> the time cometh, that whosoever killeth you,
> will think that he doeth God service.   *(16:2)*

You have read in history that some people have cut other's throats in the name of God. They think they are pleasing God, but actually they are displeasing Him. So he says: Because you do not belong to this world, people will throw you out of the synagogues and temples. Much more than that: "Whosoever killeth you, will think that he doeth God service." People will be so annoyed with you that they will go to the extent of killing you. They will think that they are the only devotees of God. Read history. We have passed through many such times. But they can kill the body only; they can never harm your soul.

> And these things will they do unto you, because
> they have not known the Father, nor me. *(16:3)*

He says: People will do these things in ignorance—they are misguided. They think they are loving God but

they do not know me at all; that is why they will try to
cut your throat. If they know the teachings of a Saint and
if they have the slightest love for the Father, they will
never become so low.

> But these things have I told you, that when the
> time shall come, ye may remember that I told
> you of them. And these things I said not unto
> you at the beginning, because I was with you.
> *(16:4)*

He says: I never prepared you for these things when
I initiated you, because I was with you. You could always turn to me for guidance. Now, since I am going to
leave you as far as my physical body is concerned, I am
trying to prepare you for the hardships that you may
have to endure because you are my disciples, so that
when they happen you may not feel hurt or offended.
Because everything has been explained to you, you will
know all these things and will be expecting this treatment from the world.

> But now I go my way to him that sent me; and
> none of you asketh me, Whither goest thou?
> *(16:5)*

He says: Do not try to hold me back. Do not tell me,
"Please do not go back to the Father! Stay with us
longer." Who would not like to go to the Father? Who
would not like to go to Him? How can you ask me to
remain away from Him?

> But because I have said these things unto you,
> sorrow hath filled your heart.   *(16:6)*

Naturally, no disciple can bear the sad news that his Master is going to leave him. It is hard for him to realize that the Master is happy to go back to his Father. Though he wants to see his Master happy, he is naturally sad over the physical separation, especially if he cannot contact the Master within himself. He is still a little child on the path. So the Master is saying these things to console his disciples.

> Nevertheless I tell you the truth; It is expedient for you that I go away: for if I go not away, the Comforter will not come unto you; but if I depart, I will send him to you.   *(16:7)*

He says: When I leave you, it will be in your interest. Hearing this, the disciple is surprised. How can it be in the interest of a disciple that the Master leave him physically? Christ explains: Day and night you are running after me now. You are mad in your love, and you are not trying to devote your time to the Spirit inside. But without attaching yourself to the Comforter, the Holy Ghost, you can never go back to the Father. So when I leave you physically, you will not find me anywhere outside and will have no option but to seek me within. Then you will be in touch with the Comforter, who will pull you up to my level, the level of the Father.

The Master comes to our level to fill us with devotion and to put us on the path, and he fills us with so much love that we cannot live without him. Physically we cannot always be with him, so the love he creates in us ultimately leads us within. When we turn within, we are in touch with the Comforter, which pulls us up to the level of the Father. "But if I depart, I will send him unto you." I am so much in love with you that my love will always be pulling you to my level.

According to history, some Saints often kept their disciples away from them for many years. It was no fault of the disciples, but it was a divine design to fill them with more longing, more love, more devotion, to prepare them for something much higher. Bulleh Shah was not allowed to go to his Master for many years.

> And when he is come, he will reprove the world
> of sin, and of righteousness, and of judgment:
> *(16:8)*

> Of sin, because they believe not on me; *(16:9)*

> Of righteousness, because I go to my Father,
> and ye see me no more; *(16:10)*

> Of judgment, because the prince of this world
> is judged. *(16:11)*

"When he is come"—once you are in touch with that Spirit or Comforter within—"he will reprove the world of sin"—then whatever sins you have committed in this world, whether during this life or even during your previous lives, will all be washed away. "And of righteousness"—you have to rise above the effect of your good karmas; good karmas also pull us back, so we have to be neither a debtor nor a creditor. "And of judgment"—then you will become worthy of the judgment of the Father, not before that. Unless you turn within, you cannot become worthy of His judgment.

> I have yet many things to say unto you, but ye
> cannot bear them now. *(16:12)*

I could tell you so much about the beauties of the inner regions and many other wonderful things, but I cannot do so now because you are not yet sufficiently advanced on the path to understand them. So far, I have given you only the simple gist of my teachings; but I shall always be with you to guide you, and I shall explain all these things to you when you reach my Radiant Form within yourself. Then you can ask me anything and I shall always reply, because then you will be able to understand.

> Howbeit when he, the Spirit of truth, is come,
> he will guide you into all truth: for he shall not
> speak of himself; but whatsoever he shall hear,
> that shall he speak: and he will shew you things
> to come. *(16:13)*

Christ says: My real form is that Word, that Spirit of Truth within yourself which comes direct from the Father. "The Spirit of truth . . . will guide you into all truth" means that the Word will lead you to the Father, who is all Truth. I have explained many things to you here, but when you come to me inside, I will show you things that you have never dreamed of and that are beyond the comprehension of the mind.

> He shall glorify me: for he shall receive of mine,
> and shall shew it unto you. *(16:14)*

The Father shall manifest my glory, for I shall have cleansed you and led you to the Father by means of the Word. And whatever instructions and guidance you are to receive, I will give you through the Word. Do not worry. I am going to leave you only as far as this physical body is concerned, but I shall always be there to guide you internally. I shall never leave you.

> All things that the Father hath are mine: there-
> fore said I, that he shall take of mine, and shall
> shew it unto you.   *(16:15)*

This is self-explanatory. Christ has often said that the Father is in him and he is in the Father. Therefore, he says, whatever I have is His and whatever He has is mine. He has simply given me this body as an instrument to help you in this world and to create love for me in your heart. And whatever love and attachment you have for me is passed on to the Father. So He will take care of mine—those who are attached to me—and will show you everything.

> A little while, and ye shall not see me: and
> again, a little while, and ye shall see me, be-
> cause I go to the Father.   *(16:16)*

Christ says: When I leave the physical body you will not be able to see me with your physical eyes, but after a little while you *shall* see me. This does not mean that you will see me with your physical eyes or that I will return to the physical body, but that your spiritual eye will be opened and you will be able to see my Radiant Form within yourself. When I shall have left this physical body, you will miss me and will long to see me. You will therefore devote more time to the spiritual practice and try to reach the point where you merge into me and into the Father, just as I have merged into the Father.

> Then said some of his disciples among them-
> selves, What is this that he saith unto us, A little
> while, and ye shall not see me: and again, a little
> while, and ye shall see me: and, Because I go to
> the Father?   *(16:17)*

They said therefore, What is this that he saith,
A little while? we cannot tell what he saith.
                                    (16:18)

Now Jesus knew that they were desirous to ask
him, and said unto them, Do ye enquire among
yourselves of that I said, A little while, and ye
shall not see me: and again, a little while, and ye
shall see me?   *(16:19)*

He says: I am saying something that is very confusing to you: after a little while, I leave you; and again
after a little while, I will be with you. He explains this:

Verily, verily, I say unto you, That ye shall weep
and lament, but the world shall rejoice; and ye
shall be sorrowful, but your sorrow shall be
turned into joy.   *(16:20)*

You will grieve when I am no longer with you in the
physical body, but that very longing will make you seek
me within yourself. However, the worldly people who
have persecuted me will be happy and rejoice that they
have gotten rid of someone whom they considered to be
a troublemaker. They are so steeped in priestcraft, dogmas, rituals, and ceremonies—not to mention their own
attachments and unfulfilled desires and indulgences in
this world—that they cannot even bear the sight of
anyone who tries to open their eyes and shake them free
of all these chains that bind them to the world. So they
persecute and malign the very person who is trying
to help them, whereas they honor, flatter, and worship
those who put stronger chains on them to bind them still
more tightly to this world.

But you have had your spiritual eye opened, and know the truth; you will therefore mourn my departure from the physical world, and this very sorrow and longing will turn into joy when you meet me within yourself and realize that I have permanently taken abode with the Father. Then you will make still more effort, which will result in your attaining the state of everlasting peace and bliss, in me and the Father.

> A woman when she is in travail hath sorrow, because her hour is come: but as soon as she is delivered of the child, she remembereth no more the anguish, for joy that a man is born into the world.   *(16:21)*

> And ye now therefore have sorrow: but I will see you again, and your heart shall rejoice, and your joy no man taketh from you.   *(16:22)*

When a woman is in labor she is usually in great pain, but the moment the child is delivered she is so happy at the birth of the child that the pain vanishes and she forgets it completely. Similarly, Christ says to his disciples, the greater your sorrow and the more you miss me when I am gone, the more effort you will make to see me within yourself, and until you achieve that goal your effort is like the anguish of a woman in labor. But your happiness will know no bounds when you meet me within yourself. Then you will absolutely forget all your trials and sorrows. You will be so filled with love, joy, and indescribable happiness that there will be no room for anything else. You will then not even remember that you were ever sad.

When we are happy in this world, even the recollection of sadness makes us feel sad. But such is the beauty of the real spiritual joy that it is not only permanent, but is so wonderful and all-absorbing that we never even bother to remember we were ever sad. There is no room for the least bit of sorrow, for we are completely enveloped in peace and contentment. We then have no unfulfilled hopes or desires, but dwell forever in perfect love, peace, and bliss beyond description.

Christ says: When you see me within yourself, you will be very happy, and no man can deprive you of this happiness. No matter how you may be persecuted or what tortures you may have to go through because of your faith in me, you will be so happy within yourself that nobody in this world could deprive you of that happiness, of that treasure of the Word.

> And in that day ye shall ask me nothing. Verily, verily, I say unto you, Whatsoever ye shall ask the Father in my name, he will give it you.
> *(16:23)*

Now, while I am still in the flesh, you have all sorts of questions and doubts. You are not even sure whether my teachings are true or just another fraud. But when you merge into my Spirit Form, the Holy Ghost, all your doubts will vanish because everything will be clear to you. And whatever you wish will be granted by the Father. When we merge into the Father, our desires are more than fulfilled and there is absolutely nothing more to wish or hope for. Whatever we may ask for has already been granted; not only that, but much more than we could ever hope for.

Christ made this statement to his new disciples who did not yet realize that by merging into the Father, everything is fulfilled. So he comforted them by saying that if you still want more, anything you ask for will be granted by the Father. But by the time we reach the Father, there is nothing left to be desired and our happiness is complete and supreme.

> Hitherto have ye asked nothing in my name: ask, and ye shall receive, that your joy may be full.   *(16:24)*

So far you have not contacted my Radiant Form within yourself and you have not asked for nor have you been ready for the real spiritual gifts, because you are still engrossed in the mind and senses. But when you make the effort for spiritual progress, you will see my Radiant Form within yourself, and then everything will be given to you automatically. Of course, you will be given only what is good for you, and you yourself will ask only for what is in your own interest. In fact, when you reach that stage you will realize that there is no need to ask for anything.

> These things have I spoken unto you in proverbs: but the time cometh, when I shall no more speak unto you in proverbs, but I shall shew you plainly of the Father.   *(16:25)*

In order to make you understand the gist of the teachings, I had to speak to you in proverbs and parables. I had to explain the spiritual in terms of the material. But when you see me within yourself, my words will be clear and direct. Then I will show you plainly what you cannot understand now. The real spiritual truths are beyond the understanding of the mind and the senses, but when you have made sufficient spiritual progress, you will know all these things by direct perception.

Truth cannot be described in mortal language. Your soul is still dominated by the mind and senses, therefore the only way I can explain it to you, according to the scope of your understanding, is by comparing it with the things familiar to you. But by following the spiritual instructions given to you by the living Master, you will come to understand more of the teachings, and eventually you will see the Truth by the direct perception of the soul.

> At that day ye shall ask in my name: and I say not unto you, that I will pray the Father for you:
> *(16:26)*

> For the Father himself loveth you, because ye have loved me, and have believed that I came out from God.　　　　　　　　　　*(16:27)*

Jesus said: Now I put off some of your questions with one excuse or another, saying that I will pray to the Father for you. But when you advance to the level where you see me within yourself, then you can ask me anything you like and I will answer you directly, because then you will be able to understand and there will be no need to put you off. But if I tried to explain some of these things to you now in mortal language, it would only confuse you rather than help you. And the Father will love you because you have had faith in me, and because you have believed that I come from God and you have loved me. As you follow the path you will know by direct perception that there is no difference between me and my Father. Now you cannot comprehend that the

Father and I are one, but then you will know, you will realize it.

> I came forth from the Father, and am come into the world: again, I leave the world, and go to the Father.   (16:28)

Here Christ says: I have come from my Father and have performed my allotted task. I have collected you into one fold; I have told you to love one another, to keep the love of the Master always alive within yourself by continuing to hear the Voice of God, so you may eventually return to the Father. Now I have finished my task and go back to Him.

17

Christ knows that he is going to be crucified and that he has finished his allotted work. He prays to the Father, and it is a beautiful prayer:

> These words spake Jesus, and lifted up his eyes to heaven, and said, Father, the hour is come; glorify thy Son, that thy Son also may glorify thee. *(17:1)*

As you know, Christ prepared his disciples by telling them that he would soon depart from this world, but that he would always be with them because he was leaving them only physically. He also reassured them that after his departure, he would send them the Holy Ghost, the Comforter. In other words, after his departure they would make more effort and would contact the Spirit, or Sound Current, which is always resounding within every one of us.

After finishing his allotted task in this world, Christ asks his Father to glorify him by taking him back to Himself. This is the way the Father glorifies the Son, and the Son glorifies the Father by always praising the Father, by filling his disciples with love and devotion for Him.

> As thou hast given him power over all flesh, that he should give eternal life to as many as thou hast given him. *(17:2)*

Saints do not give eternal life to everybody. Only a certain number of souls that are designated to be redeemed by a particular Master are allotted to him by the Father. To those he gives eternal life.

> And this is life eternal, that they might know thee the only true God, and Jesus Christ, whom thou hast sent.   *(17:3)*

That eternal life is to know the Father and to merge back in Him through His Son, the living Master, who at that time was Jesus Christ.

> I have glorified thee on the earth: I have finished the work which thou gavest me to do. *(17:4)*

I have filled my disciples with love and devotion for You. They had forgotten You by being in love with the perishable world, but now I have turned their faces towards You. "I have finished the work which thou gavest me to do." He does not say that he can save any souls after his death. He says: I have done my allotted task; I have nothing more to do in this world.

Like all true Masters, Christ was in constant communication with the Father and naturally did not have to express himself in spoken words. Everything that Jesus said to his Father was for the benefit of his disciples. He knew, and his Father knew, that his task was finished and that he was now going to merge back in the Father, but he said all this for the sake of his disciples, to comfort and console them.

> And now, O Father, glorify thou me with thine own self with the glory which I had with thee before the world was.   *(17:5)*

I have finished my work. So, Father, take me back to Yourself, where I was before I came here. Take me back to where we were before You made this world, before the creation began. I was with You then and I want to come back to You now, because my task here is finished.

> I have manifested thy name unto the men which thou gavest me out of the world: thine they were, and thou gavest them me; and they have kept thy word. *(17:6)*

I have created love and devotion for You in the souls You have allotted to me, says Christ. They were Yours to begin with, before the creation, but then they became lost in this world, and You gave them to me to lead them back to You. Now they have been attached to Your Word—the Shabd, or Nam—and are on the path leading back to You.

> Now they have known that all things whatsoever thou hast given me are of thee. *(17:7)*

Now that they are attached to the Word, they realize that nothing belongs to them, that their worldly possessions, friends, relatives, their own body and soul—everything comes from You and is Yours. They are in love with the Creator and not His creation. They are in love with the Giver and not the gifts He has bestowed upon them. They appreciate the gifts and are grateful for all Your blessings, but they are not attached to them. They are attached to You alone through the Master, Your Son, whom You have sent into this world to take them back to You.

> For I have given unto them the words which
> thou gavest me; and they have received them,
> and have known surely that I came out from
> thee, and they have believed that thou didst
> send me. *(17:8)*

I have given them the words, the teachings, which You gave me for them, and I have attached them to the Word which they have received—or rather, the awareness of which they have received—through me. Now they have faith that I came from You and that You sent me into this world.

> I pray for them: I pray not for the world, but for
> them which thou hast given me; for they are
> thine. *(17:9)*

Christ says: I pray only for the souls You have allotted to my care. They already belong to You; I am merely leading them back to You. I do not pray for the world and the people of the world because that is not my concern. I do not interfere in the affairs of the world. I have done only that for which You sent me here, and that is to guide these particular souls back to You.

> And all mine are thine, and thine are mine; and I
> am glorified in them. *(17:10)*

Whatever is mine is actually Yours, says Christ, and since You and I are one, whatever is Yours is mine. Originally, these souls were Yours, were with You, and now they are on the path back to You. Since I have attached them to the Word and put them on the path, I am also glorified in them because of their love and devotion for You.

> And now I am no more in the world, but these
> are in the world, and I come to thee. Holy
> Father, keep through thine own name those
> whom thou hast given me, that they may be
> one, as we are. *(17:11)*

I am going to leave this world and come back to You,
but my disciples, whom I have put on the path leading
back to You, will remain here. Holy Father, shower
Your grace on them and keep them on the path, so that
they may merge in You and become one with You, even
as You and I are one.

> While I was with them in the world, I kept them
> in thy name: those that thou gavest me I have
> kept, and none of them is lost. . . . *(17:12)*

Jesus says: While I was with them in the world, I
kept them in Your love and devotion by attaching them
to the Word and giving them the guidance they needed.
Not a single one of those You gave me has been lost. But
now they will not have my physical guidance, so please
have mercy on them, ever keep Your guiding hand over
them and bless them, that they may not go astray on
their way back to You.

> And now come I to thee; and these things I
> speak in the world, that they might have my joy
> fulfilled in themselves. *(17:13)*

The living Master is speaking these words openly
for the benefit of his disciples, so that they may be
reassured that they will be looked after when their
Master leaves this world. Their joy will be fulfilled
because they know that their Master is eager and happy

to merge back into the Father in heaven, and that they
also will ultimately merge into Him.

> I have given them thy word; and the world hath
> hated them, because they are not of the world,
> even as I am not of the world.   *(17:14)*

Now that I have attached them to the Word, the
worldly people hate them because they are no longer
interested in the worldly people or in the pleasures and
possessions of this world. Even as I do not belong to
this world, they also are not of this world, for now they
are on the path leading back to You. Take care of them,
because the world naturally hates them.

> I pray not that thou shouldest take them out of
> the world, but that thou shouldest keep them
> from the evil.   *(17:15)*

Christ says: I am not praying that they should all die
now and go to You at once, because they have yet to
clear their karmas, their sins. I do not pray that You take
them before they are ready. I pray only that Kal, Satan,
the negative power, may not lead them astray.

> They are not of the world, even as I am not of
> the world.   *(17:16)*

> Sanctify them through thy truth: thy word is
> truth.   *(17:17)*

They are not attached to this creation anymore—
even as I am not attached to it. Make them pure through
the grace of Your Word. This Word is true because it is
real and eternal. It will never perish.

As thou hast sent me into the world, even so
have I also sent them into the world. *(17:18)*

And for their sakes I sanctify myself, that they
also might be sanctified through the truth.
(17:19)

Neither pray I for these alone, but for them also
which shall believe on me through their word;
(17:20)

That they all may be one; as thou, Father, art in
me, and I in thee, that they also may be one in
us: that the world may believe that thou hast
sent me. *(17:21)*

In the previous chapters Jesus gave instructions to
his disciples to preach and share with others the teachings that he had given them. He briefed them on how to
conduct themselves with the seekers: they should *live*
the teachings, not merely preach them.

Jesus says: I have sanctified myself by merging myself in the Word, or Truth, so that my disciples may also
be sanctified through it. I pray to You, O Father, not
only for myself and my disciples but also for those who
will be brought on the path through my disciples. I pray
that they will live in the teachings by attaching themselves to the Word, so that ultimately all may become
one as You and I have become one and as my disciples
and I have become one.

And the glory which thou gavest me I have
given them; that they may be one, even as we
are one: *(17:22)*

I in them, and thou in me, that they may be
made perfect in one; and that the world may

> know that thou hast sent me, and hast loved
> them, as thou hast loved me.   *(17:23)*

Here again Jesus Christ emphasizes the oneness of his disciples with himself and the Father—and not only that, but also the oneness of his successors and their disciples with himself and the Father. So in essence, they are all one in the Father through the Word, for He is realized only by merging ourselves in the Word, the Shabd, which is God. Christ asks that they all may be made perfect, for only then can they be united in Him.

So he says: O Father, as You are perfect, I have become perfect by merging in You. I pray that my disciples may also be made perfect by merging in me and then, through me, in You. Then the world may believe that You have sent me. As You have loved me, so I have loved them.

The meaning of Christ's words here is that when the disciple becomes perfect, pure, or whole, then his Master is automatically honored by his living example. So the best way to share the teachings of our Master with any seeker is to become a shining example of those very teachings. By living the teachings, the disciple becomes perfect and merges back in the Father through his Master.

> Father, I will that they also, whom thou hast
> given me, be with me where I am; that they may
> behold my glory, which thou hast given me: for
> thou lovedst me before the foundation of the
> world.   *(17:24)*

Jesus continues his prayer to the Father, saying: I pray that all the souls whom You have entrusted to my care will be with me where I am, so that they may know

that You love them as you love me, as You loved me
even before the creation of the world. The Father loved
every soul before the creation, because every soul was
with the Father. This same love—this Word, Shabd, or
Nam—is attracting us, the marked souls, back to Him,
and we will finally merge in Him and become as we were
before the creation. Then he says:

> O righteous Father, the world hath not known
> thee: but I have known thee, and these have
> known that thou hast sent me.   *(17:25)*

People believe that they are worshipping God, but
they do not really know what they are worshipping. In
fact, they are being deceived by the negative power,
who will further ensnare and entangle them in this
world again and again. The negative power tricks them
into thinking that they are worshipping the Father and
thus prevents them from contacting a living Master, so
that they may not know and worship the one true God.
But I have known You, says Christ, and those whom I
have initiated love and worship You and know that You
have sent me.

Until we contact a living Master who has realized
God, we can never realize the Father. How can we
worship something we have not seen? Unless the Father
comes to our level in the flesh, in the garb of a living
Master—as Jesus was for his disciples—we can never
know anything about our Father—least of all, how to
worship Him. Jesus says: My disciples have known me,
that is, they believe that I am the Word made flesh, that I
have been sent by You to their level and that You have
merged in me and I have merged in You. By worshipping me, they are now worshipping You.

And I have declared unto them thy name, and
will declare it: that the love wherewith thou hast
loved me may be in them, and I in them. *(17:26)*

I have attached them to Your Name, your Word,
Your Shabd, Your Nam. They are filled with my love
and I am filled with Your love. In the same way they are
all filled with Your love. So take them ultimately to You.
I want all to reach where I am going now.

CONCLUSION

EVERY SAINT tells us about the relationship of the soul with the Lord. The soul is a particle of the Lord. We are separated from that Ocean and have taken the company of the mind, and the mind is already a victim of the senses. Whatever karmas, or actions, the mind does, being a slave of the senses, the soul also has to pay for them—it has to reap the fruit of those actions. During our lifetime we do both good and bad deeds. Whether the deeds are good or bad, the results of both bring us back into this world, and we are brought back into that form of life in which we can best bear the consequences of all our actions. Then, while we are going through the results of our actions, we are also continually performing new actions. So we continue to come and go, but always remain in this prison of "eighty-four," the eight million four hundred thousand species of life.

The human form is given to us to enable us to escape from this prison and go up and merge back into the Lord. He, whom we want to see and into whom we want to go back and merge, is nowhere outside. He is within us. Every Saint, every Master, has tried to explain to us that the human body is the abode of the Lord, or God— as Christ says, "the temple of the living God." Guru Nanak calls it the place where the Lord resides. *Rishis* and *munis* have referred to it as the body in which the Lord lives and in which our soul can become the Lord again by merging back into Him. Every Saint has taught this simple truth that the Lord is within every one of us. If He is within, naturally we have to seek Him within. In order to meet the Lord we have to research within ourbody. The human body is the laboratory in which we have to make this research to attain union with Him.

Our spiritual journey starts from the soles of our feet and ends at the top of our head. In the body, the seat of the soul and mind, knotted together, is in the center behind our eyes. Some people call it *til,* which is a small seed. Others call it "the door" of our house. And yet others refer to it as the third eye or, as Christ calls it in the Bible, the single eye. Whatever we may call it, this point is the seat of the soul and the mind knotted together. From here our consciousness is scattered in the whole world through the nine apertures of the body— the two eyes, the two ears, the two nostrils, the mouth, and the two lower outlets. But even being here at the thinking center, we are not here. Our thoughts are spread into the whole world. We are always thinking about something. Something is always moving about before our mind's eye. If you close your eyes, you are not here. Your mind is never still. You are thinking about your children or your work or your business. Whatever we are thinking of appears in our mind so that we contemplate on that form. Thus our entire consciousness has spread into the whole world.

The first step on the spiritual journey is to withdraw our consciousness back to the eye center. Christ mystically referred to this process when he said, "Knock, and it shall be opened unto you."[1] We always knock from the outside, and the door of the house is always opened from inside. The Lord is inside and we are outside. We have to knock from the outside so that the door leading to our house may be opened. This knock-

---

1. *Matt. 7:7.*

ing at the door of our house consists of bringing our consciousness back to the eye center. When we bring it here the door opens; the third eye, or single eye, is opened.

Then it is stated in the Bible: "Seek, and ye shall find."[1] When the door opens, we seek that path leading to our home. Once we are on that path, we find the Lord for whom we were making our research. So unless we withdraw back by concentrating at the eye center, we cannot follow the spiritual path, we cannot complete the journey. The eye center being the seat of the soul and mind knotted together, it is from here that our mind is being pulled down by the senses. Our mind is fond of pleasures, so it is constantly running down from the eye center to the senses to seek pleasures. But unless our mind gets something better than the sense pleasures, it will not cease from running downwards.

Saints explain to us that here at the eye center is the Word, the Audible Life Stream, the Sound Current, the Shabd, the Nam. Saints have given different names to that Sound, to that Silent Music, to that Power. Christ refers to it as the Word, the Logos, the Sound, the Holy Ghost. And that Audible Life Stream, or Word, Shabd, Nam, Logos—whatever name you give it—is within every one of us at the eye center. Unless we withdraw to this point, we cannot be in touch with it. And that Sound is so fascinating, so charming, so tempting, that once we are attached to it, we are automatically detached from the senses. Only attachment can create detachment within us. Detachment never creates any attachment within us. Once we withdraw our consciousness to the Word, or Logos, attachment to it automatically

---

1. Ibid.

detaches us from the senses. Thus we start on our spiritual journey.

Christ says, "If therefore thine eye be single, thy whole body shall be full of light."[1] So when we open the single eye, the third eye, "the door" of our house, then we see that Light. With the help of that Light we have to travel on the path. With the help of that Sound we have to know the direction in which we are to travel.

Suppose we leave our house and go out for a long walk in the evening; it becomes pitch dark and we forget the direction of our house—whether we have left it to the right or to the left or whether it is in front of us or behind us. We generally stand quietly in the darkness and try to hear some sound coming from the direction of our house. It may be of our television, it may be the barking of dogs, it may be people talking. With the help of the sound, we try to know the direction of our house. But after we catch the sound and have found the direction of our house, then another obstacle is still in our way—the darkness. There may be someone else's yard in our way, there may be thorny bushes, uneven ground, or a pond; but if we have a light in our hand, then with the help of that light and that sound we come back to our destination which we had lost.

Similarly, the Lord is within every one of us but we have completely forgotten the path leading back to Him. He has kept Sound within us and He has kept Light within us. With the help of the Sound we have to know the direction of the Lord's house, and with the help of its Light we have to travel on the path leading to our home. That is why Sound and Light are both mentioned in the Bible. These are the two fundamental

---

1. *Matt. 6:22.*

things which are essential for us to go back to the Lord.
That is why Christ says, "If thine eye be single, thy
whole body shall be full of light."

At present, if we close our eyes, we see nothing but
darkness inside. But when we open that single eye by
withdrawing our consciousness to the eye center, then
instead of darkness, we see that Light within and we get
real bliss and peace. We have to merge into that Light.
And with the help of that Sound and Light we come
back to our home.

Christ says, "In my Father's house are many mansions."[1] The journey is not just straight. We have to pass
through many stages with the help of the Sound and
with the help of the Light, before we can go back to our
own home.

But these are not the teachings only of Christ. Every
Saint who has come from that home, who has traveled
back to that destination, has the same message to give,
has the same teachings to impart. No Saint comes into
this world to create a religion, to divide human beings,
to set one nation against another, to set one religion
against another religion. They come to tell us the real
mystic teachings—the way, the path, the Truth which
leads us back to our own home. Generally, after the
Saints go, people do not know what to do. So they form
organizations; somebody takes them over for his own
selfish ends, and thus a religion is formed. Then we
become bigoted, we start quarrelling amongst ourselves and completely forget the real teachings of the
Saints.

Every Saint has the same message to give; every
Saint has the same teachings to explain to us, and it

makes no difference whether he is in the East or the West. It is simple logic that if the Lord is one and He is within every one of us and if we have to seek Him within our body, then the path leading to our destination, to our home, cannot be two. It must be one. So it is impossible even to think that there can be one path leading to the Lord's house for Christians, another for Hindus, another for Sikhs, and still another for Muslims. There may be a difference in our interpretation or in our understanding, but there cannot be two paths leading to His house. If we seek Him within, we all will find the same path, and that is of Sound and Light. But if we search for Him outside, then everybody has his own path; then it is impossible to come together.

It is only on a spiritual basis that we can come together and be near to each other. Then we experience real brotherhood and enjoy real peace and bliss. But if we are searching outside, if we are seeking Him in different directions, then we are driven away from one another. As I have said many times, the nearer we are to the Lord, the nearer we are to one another. The farther we are from Him, the farther we are driven away from one another.

In order to find peace we have to undertake research within ourselves. We must have a spiritual outlook. A political, economic, and social outlook can never give us peace. They will improve our physical environment, they will improve our standard of living, but perhaps in the long run these things will make us even more unhappy and frustrated.

Real peace and happiness we can get only from within ourselves. Unless we make an effort within to seek that real peace, we can never get it. The nearer we are towards our home, towards our destination, towards the Lord, the greater the peace and happiness we will find within ourselves. The more we wander away from Him, the more frustrated and unhappy we become every day.

I think that this is just a gist of the teachings of Jesus Christ and of all Saints. You may read the Bhagavad Gita, you may read the Adi Granth, you may read the Bible, you may read the mystic works of the Muslim Saints, you may read the teachings of any Mystic, and you will find that every Saint has the same message to give.

But in most cases this message has been obscured by rituals, ceremonies, and dogmas introduced by the priestly class. After a Saint departs, the people forget the real practice—they forget how to seek the Lord within the body. So another Saint comes to remind us of the same path to the one God. He gives us the same truth, the same teachings that have been obscured by the dogmas, rituals, and ceremonies. The teaching of the Saints is not a new faith, not a new religion. It is a science, so to say. It is a practice, a method, by which we have to bring back our consciousness to the eye center and then travel on the spiritual path back to our home, our source, the Lord himself.

If with an unbiased mind we make a research in the teachings of any Saint, wherever he may be born in this world and at whatever time, we will always find the same Truth—the base and the foundation of all religions. We should be more concerned with that Truth which will liberate us from our sins, from birth and death, instead of unnecessarily wasting our time by giving importance to the coverings of rituals and ceremonies. Those things only mislead and misguide us by taking our attention away from the very purpose of life on this earth. As you know, that purpose is to reap the harvest which is ready for us and thus return to the Father on the path which He himself has put within us.

QUESTIONS AND ANSWERS

After completing his discourses on Saint John during his tours abroad and at the meetings in the International Guest House at the Dera, the Master indicated that if anyone desired to ask any questions, he was most welcome to do so. Following are some of those questions and the Master's answers:

1 **Q.** Maharaj Ji, in the Communion service of the Christian Church, how does the drinking of wine and the eating of bread tie up with Sant Mat?

A. As I have just told you, these are the rituals and ceremonies to which we have become victims. The wine is the living water inside; the bread is the Shabd and Nam. He says, "I am the bread of life,"[1] and what is "I"? The Word made flesh, the Shabd, or Nam. So Shabd is the bread and the living water is the blood. Communion is to be in touch with Shabd, to be in touch with the Word inside. To drink that water of life outside is nothing but ritual and ceremony.

2 **Q.** I should like to know how one can have peace and longing at the same time. In Sant Mat, right from the beginning, again and again, we are told we will only find peace inside. One experiences longing to see the Master inside, which increases, and I believe that when one has met the Master inside, the longing is even greater. How is it possible to have peace and longing at the same time?

---

1. *John 6:35.*

A.   Sister, that very longing, that very devotion, gives one peace and bliss. One would not like to live without that longing and without that devotion for the Master. Actually, that is peace, that is the love that detaches us from everything in the world and attaches us to Shabd and Nam, the Master. Detaching yourself from the world and attaching yourself to the Master—the Sound, or Shabd, inside—gives you peace and happiness.

> *3* **Q.**   Maharaj Ji, giving to the Master body, mind, and wealth seems almost an impossible thing. What conditions would there be before the satsangi can do that?

A.   Brother, Master never actually accepts a single pie[1] from any disciple and, if he accepts, he is not a Master. "Giving wealth, body, and mind to the Master" means thinking that everything belongs to the Master, nothing belongs to me in this world. I am only a puppet. Whatever he wants me to do in this world, I will do. This wealth belongs to him. Just as an agent spends money on his master's wishes, on whatever the Master wants you to spend you should spend it. The agent pays the bills on behalf of his master. So, think not of this wealth which you have acquired as yours. Think that it has been given to you by the Master and you are only spending it on his behalf. Thus you will become detached from it. Use it as his.

And giving our minds to the Master means keeping our minds within the commandments which have been given to us at the time of initiation, not compromising with those principles—this is giving our minds to the

---

1. *Pie:* formerly a small bronze coin of India, equal to ¹⁄₁₉₂ of a rupee.

Master—not allowing our attention to become scattered.

Giving our body to the Master means rendering service with the body. You see, this body is filled with ego, and to serve the creation of the Creator will create humility. Think that this body is not yours. When you think of it as yours, you want people to praise you, to honor you, to give you glory—then ego comes into it. Think humbly that this does not belong to you; this belongs to the Father; so we should use it as His and not ours.

Use it as if it belongs to the Master, then you will not do evil deeds with it. So be of service to His devotees, to His creation. This is using our body as if it belongs to the Master. Master neither needs our body nor needs our mind nor needs our wealth. This is for our own spiritual progress.

4 Q. Maharaj Ji, does one, then, do this to create a habit, or does it require certain elevation of the spirit to enable one to do that?

A. I think actually it requires elevation, spiritual experience. Unless we advance inside spiritually, just merely by thinking, we cannot acquire this. We have to be advanced and have spiritual experiences to feel all that. Mere thinking or analyzing these things does not solve the problem.

5 Q. Master, what can we applicants do in the interim period, while waiting for initiation, to help us in concentration—to do something actively?

A. Brother, we hold group meetings here, as you all know, and we have so many books on the science. You should try to read these books, try to satisfy your intellect; and if still you have any questions, you are most welcome to ask satsangi brothers or to write to me. Make up your mind that these are the teachings for you; satisfy your intellect. That is all you are supposed to do meanwhile.

6 Q.   Maharaj Ji, in meditation is there a stage on the path where the *surat* and *nirat* must become one at the same time, when one sees and hears at the same time?

A.   Actually, as I explained at a meeting one day, *surat* is the power of the soul to hear, and the power of the soul to see is *nirat*. It is one and the same thing. Now, you have eyes and you have ears. When you hear anybody, you also see him. It is not a case of first seeing and then hearing. As you have eyes and ears, similarly the soul has an internal eye and an internal ear. You will hear the Sound and you will also see the Light. Ultimately, Sound and Light become one. They are one, they are not two. They merge back into one. Light comes from the Sound.

Q.   But in the beginning, Maharaj Ji, you try to see the one or hear the other?

A.   Some disciples first see the Light, they start with the Light, and then hear the Sound. Some people hear the Sound first and then see the Light. There is very little difference. Ultimately they both become one.

7 Q.   Maharaj Ji, very often you tell us that we must not worry. When we write to you, your reply is very, very often, and repeatedly, "Do not worry."

Can you elaborate as to why it is unnecessary for
us to worry?

A. Brother, I am sorry to say that we are generally in
the habit of creating problems, and when we cannot
solve them we become frustrated and we start worrying. But there is no necessity to create problems at all.
You see, it is the mind which is always creating problems and then it takes pleasure in solving them. When
we cannot solve them, we become unhappy. There is no
necessity to worry, because whatever is destined, whatever has to happen, has already happened, is already
destined. We will have to face it. Nobody can solve the
problems of the world, but with meditation we can rise
above the problems. It is very difficult to collect the
thorns of this world, but you can definitely put on strong
shoes so that the thorns and thistles do not bother you at
all. So meditation will drive out worry from you; it will
help you to face the world. It will help you to rise above
the problems; it will help you to go through your destiny
cheerfully. That is why I always try to advise that you
should attend to meditation and not worry.

8 **Q.** Maharaj Ji, if one manages to sit for a fair
amount of time in meditation without successfully
concentrating, how does this help one?

A. Brother, if a child will not start learning to walk, he
will never be able to walk. He does not succeed in
walking in one day. You see, we have to put an effort
into it. Even if we fail, we have to put in more effort. In
the face of our failures, we have to put in more and more
effort. It is a lifelong struggle. Ultimately we succeed,
but we become impatient, we do not know how much

karma we have to clear. Every little bit of time that we
devote to our meditation, we are definitely making progress of which we are not conscious at all. Do not think
that we are not making progress if we are unable to
experience or see inside. We have definitely made progress, whatever time we devote to meditation. So we
should not be impatient. We should try to give our time
regularly and punctually to simran and bhajan.

> 9 **Q.** Maharaj Ji, in the sangat there seems to be
> great confusion about meat. A certain lady asked
> me the other day what her position is. Her hus-
> band demands that the children eat meat. She
> herself does not eat meat. What karma is she creat-
> ing? Somebody went back to White River and said
> that we have to get rid of all our pets because every
> time we buy meat for the pets (dogs and cats) we
> are creating karma. Somebody else got the same
> impression if we buy meat for the servants. They
> will not work in a home where they are not pro-
> vided with meat. A number of these servants live
> far from butchers and very often, when they do
> go to a butcher, the butcher exploits them. Now,
> could we have a directive from you? What is the
> position about a satsangi living in a home where
> meat has to be provided?

A. I know it is very difficult for you people who live in
the West to abstain to that extent to which we should
abstain from eating meat, but we have to take a practical
view of life. First, we ourselves should never eat meat at
all in any circumstances, and if we can avoid serving
anybody, we should try to avoid it. If we cannot avoid it
with all our efforts and cannot help it, then we may
serve. But that does not mean that those who can avoid
it should not do so. They should try to avoid as much as

possible either serving it to anybody or handling it. However, if still you cannot avoid it, then do not eat it yourself. That is the only practical view I can suggest.

10 **Q.** Maharaj Ji, concerning the process of forgiving a harm done to one, I imagine that one could have harmed and forgotten the harm done, and therefore would not be able to recall it in order to forgive. Can that particular situation arise?

A. If you have injured somebody and you are fortunate enough to have forgotten it, it is all right, but generally we never forget what harm we do to others, and if this is weighing on our conscience then we should try to ask for forgiveness. If we have not consciously harmed anybody, then we should try to devote our time to meditation. That also squares up that karma.

11 **Q.** Maharaj Ji, we are aware sometimes of a great deal of what we would call primitive tribes living outside the understanding of our Western civilization, yet we are also aware that they have consciousness of God, whether it may be the worship of the sun, or some image, because probably they know no better—does that bring them closer to God-realization?

A. No matter what we say of the primitive tribes, most civilized people are much further away from God than the primitive tribes. Why pity them? Why not pity the civilized ones, who have the intelligence, who have the knowledge, and yet they do not understand that they are far away from God.

Q. Maharaj Ji, what is not clear to me is, if they worship the sun, which is part of creation, as a symbol of God, are they in fact worshipping God?

A.   Christ has just explained that unless you worship God "in spirit," you do not worship Him at all. Unless you attach yourself to the Word, or Nam, there is no worship of the Father at all. He says: Since you have come to me now, now you will learn how to worship God. To worship God is to worship Him "in spirit," in the Word, or Nam, so whatever you may do, unless you are attached to the Holy Ghost, or Shabd, inside, you are not worshipping the Father at all. Whether you belong to a primitive tribe or whether you are in a civilized country, it makes no difference.

12   **Q.**   John talks about Christ as his successor, and we have learned that there has been a succession of Masters ever since the world was created, but Saint John never mentions any Master of his.

A.   The reason for that can be that the New Testament has been written by the disciples of Christ, so they start from John onward. If it had been written by John the Baptist himself, he would have started from his own Master or from more predecessors; but this is written by Christ's disciples and even by disciples of Christ's successors. They are concerned only with Christ and his teachings, and incidentally they refer to John the Baptist because John the Baptist initiated Christ. It does not mean that John the Baptist had no Master. It may not have been mentioned because it was unnecessary.

Q.   I have heard that some people see the projection of their own Master in the successor.

A.   Slowly and slowly they realize that their own Master has been manifested in his successor. They get proof from within and also from outside. But that personal association and bond that they have created with their own Master cannot leave so easily. That does not leave.

13 **Q.** Master, why do we need to be concerned with what past Masters have said when we have a living Master now?

A. Unless we are convinced that the same teachings have been given by past Masters, we will never believe in the teachings of the living Master. We have faith in the living Master only when we are convinced that the teachings of the past Masters are coming through him. If every Master explained his teachings without referring to the past Masters, nobody would believe him.

As you have read, Christ referred to Moses and to John the Baptist because people were looking to them for guidance, and he had to interpret their teachings rightly to those people. Only then were they convinced and became his disciples. In the same way, people are looking to Christ today. They have to be told what Christ's teachings are, otherwise they will not listen to the present Mystics.

People have to be told what Guru Nanak's real teachings are or what Kabir's real teachings are, because by tradition, by birth, they have faith in those past Mystics. From early life they have been taught to believe the teachings of those Mystics. You will never be convinced about any living Master's teachings without reference to the past. It is impossible. That is why the Adi Granth was compiled. People used to tell the successor that his teachings seemed new, and he had to convince the audience that what he was saying or what Guru Nanak had said was nothing new, that the same teachings had been given by earlier Mystics—by Kabir, by Farid, and by other Mystics whose writings have been included in the Adi Granth. When people became convinced that their present Guru's teachings were the same as those given by earlier Mystics, they placed their faith in him.

Without reference to the past, maybe only one in a million will straightaway put faith in the present Master—hardly one in a million. Everybody is looking to the past, to the traditional teachings, because they have been brought up that way. Their mind has been conditioned in that atmosphere, in those teachings, by inheritance, by family tradition, by religious tradition.

Soami Ji, in his lifetime, always held satsangs from the Adi Granth. He never gave his own sermons without reference to the book of another Mystic. He could have straightaway given his own teachings—"This is my teaching; follow it." But no. Read his writings. He is always saying: I am not giving you new teachings. Christ also says: Not a jot or tittle can be changed or added.[1] The teachings belong to my Father and they are as old as my Father.

Q.   What about after our becoming satsangis?

A.   But there is a big jump to make before we become a satsangi, and for that jump we need the teachings of the past Masters. Even after becoming a satsangi we always need confirmation that what we are following is really right. The mind is shaky and wavering, and we feel convinced of the teachings only when we see that they

---

1. "Till heaven and earth pass, one jot or one tittle shall in no wise pass from the law, till all be fulfilled" (*Matt. 5:18*).

are the same as those of past Mystics. But once we
achieve spiritual experience, we do not bother about the
books. That is something different.

14 Q. You tell us that if a satsangi does his daily
duty, devotion to simran and bhajan, he becomes
a better person, a better Christian, a better Jew, a
better Muslim. But would it not be better for a
satsangi to renounce all outward religions?

A. What is the definition of a better Christian? One
who follows the real teachings of Christ. Do we not
become better Christians when we understand Sant
Mat, the teachings of the Saints? Then we understand
the real teachings of Christ: the purpose of this human
birth, the purpose of Christ's coming into this world, the
law that he has given us which governs the soul's return
to the Creator. When we understand his teachings in the
right perspective and try to follow them with our best
intentions and efforts, do we not become better Christians?

It is very difficult—I do not know what a Christian's
definition of a true Christian is, because there are seven-
ty or eighty schools of thought in Christianity; they all
call themselves Christians and yet denounce one another. But to me, the real Christian is one who follows
the real teachings of Christ; he may belong to any race,
caste, or creed; it is not important. He becomes a better
follower of Soami Ji Maharaj, he becomes a better follower of Guru Nanak, because all the Mystics have the
same teachings. They have the same spiritual Truth to
share with us. So naturally you become a better seeker.
And you can take any label—whether you are a better
Sikh, or a better Christian, or a better Muslim, or a

better Hindu is immaterial. You become a better human being because you honestly begin to understand the teachings and try to follow them.

When the living guide or teacher is no more, then the people try to hold on to the shell. They try to arrest the teachings into some organization and to live by dogmas, rituals, and ceremonies, because the poor people have nothing else to hold on to. What else can they do? And then, the priestly class is very clever. They always like to exploit our religious feeling. They lead us astray through one ritual or the other, and we live in the belief that we are following a certain Mystic. Actually we go far, far away from the Mystic's real teachings. The priestly class becomes so powerful in the organized religions that it becomes very difficult even to suggest anything to them. What happened to Christ? The same thing. He wanted to tell the Jews the real teaching of John the Baptist, the real teaching of Moses, but they could not tolerate it.

The Romans who crucified Christ did so to satisfy the religious leadership of the Jews. It was the priestly class who made the Romans sacrifice his life. It is plainly stated in the Bible that the chief priests and the Pharisees sent a band of men and officers to arrest Jesus and take him away.[1] We also find in the Bible that it was the chief priests and the officers who aroused the mob by crying out, "Crucify him, crucify him."[2] It was the priests and the Pharisees who thought he was coming into conflict with their bread and butter, when he was only trying to explain to the people the real teaching of Moses. He never told them he was laying the foundation

---

1. *John 18:3.*
2. *John 19:6.*

of Christianity or any new religion. He was giving them the real teaching of the Mystic.

And the same thing is happening even now. Christ's teachings have been forgotten and distorted, and the priestly classes are exploiting the people. It is so with every religion. The priestly class of all religions is more concerned with filling their pockets and meeting their own selfish ends rather than with the teachings of any Mystic.

The real Mystics and the real seekers go beyond these organizations. They do not confine themselves to these traditions. They are all waves of the same Ocean, whether a wave of that Ocean has come as Christ, as Soami Ji, as Guru Nanak, as Buddha, or as any other Mystic.

15 **Q.** When Christ says he will raise at the last day only those people who have seen him, is it possible that he was referring to seeing him in a vision?

A. Actually, he is explaining: Who are my disciples that I am going to raise at the last day? That is the subject he is explaining, and he makes the answer clear: those who see me and believe in me. So you have to take seeing first—that will be the physical seeing—and then believing. You do not put your belief in a Master after seeing his Radiant Form. You have to believe in him and work according to his teachings to reach that level of consciousness. So you have to take it systematically.

And then he is explaining in this context the necessity of a living Master. He is saying: Moses cannot help you, John the Baptist cannot help you, because you have not seen them; they are accusing you to the Father; they have written about me in the scriptures. Continu-

ing in the same vein, he is explaining who his disciples
are. So you have to read this with reference to what you
have read earlier in the Bible. It shows that this seeing is
a physical seeing.

> *16* **Q.**   Maharaj Ji, at the time of initiation, the Mas-
> ter takes charge of the soul of the initiate and takes
> the entire account of karmas of the initiate from
> Kal and transfers it to the Master. At the time of
> death, the soul has to pass through the path where
> the Master is. So the question of the Master's not
> coming to receive the soul does not arise.

A.   Every mother loves her child. There cannot be a
greater bond of love than that between the mother and
son, but if the son is naughty, if he does not behave
properly, the mother does not spare him a spanking.
She spanks the child, not because she hates the child
but because she loves him. Just to set him right, to make
him a model, she spanks him, she scolds him, she beats
him. Similarly, if we do not behave as a good disciple,
we are not forsaken by the Master, but are definitely
disciplined and reproved.

No mother will turn her child over to the police, no
matter what crime he may commit, but she never spares
the child from a thrashing. If the child is dirty, the
mother will not lift him till she gives him a bath and
makes him clean. Only then will she take him in her lap.
She will never throw the child on the roadside or send
him to the police or turn him out of the house. So if we
are dirty, full of sins, we have to be washed. How the
Master cleanses us is his job. He does not turn us over
to the negative power, but we have to be cleansed before
we can be in his lap again.

17 Q.   When we backbite and judge others, do we
give away the credit of our meditation?

A.   Well, sister, this creates sort of an ego in us. When
we malign somebody, backbite somebody, we think we
are much superior to the other person. We are building
ego in ourselves, and ego stands in our way.

Q.   Maharaj Ji, why is it so easy for us to criticize
and judge and hurt other people and so difficult for
us to admit our own shortcomings?

A.   Christ said in the Bible very clearly that we do not
see the beam in our own eyes, but we are anxious to see
a speck or mote in another person's eyes.[1] We do not sit
in judgment on ourselves, but we are always anxious to
sit in judgment on others. We do not look within; we
always look at others, at how they behave. We never try
to see what we are, how we behave, where we stand; we
are only concerned with where other people stand. We
want them to be perfect, but we do not want ourselves
to be perfect. Actually, we love them and we hate ourselves, because we do not want to make ourselves perfect. We are not concerned with ourselves. We are
concerned only with others. We are obsessed with them
or we are attached to them. Even by hatred we are
attached to them, and we are not attached to ourselves,
so we do not try to look within.

We must love ourselves. We must sit in judgment on
ourselves. We must make ourselves whole, we must
make ourselves pure. If you will go on judging yourself,

---

1. "Any why beholdest thou the mote that is in thy brother's eye, but
considerest not the beam that is in thine own eye? Or how wilt thou say to
thy brother, Let me pull out the mote out of thine eye; and, behold, a beam
is in thine own eye?" *(Matt. 7:3–4)*

you will never get any time to judge anybody else. We have so much on which to judge and improve ourselves.

18 **Q.** If the disciple has made very little progress but has definite faith that his Master is perfect —

A. Well, brother, this faith does not come without meditation. If you are trying to find a solution, that without meditation you can get all these things, it is impossible. Real faith you can never build without meditation. This intellectual faith many times you build, and many times it is destroyed. But once you see the Radiant Form of the Master within and you make spiritual progress, then even if the whole world tries to dissuade you from the path, you will not leave the path. That is faith.

Faith does not mean the intellectual faith that we generally try to build and think that there is no need for meditation. Without meditation you cannot get real faith. Intellectual faith can be deceptive. Faith gained from experience is the main thing. Then if the whole world is against you, you are not shaken. You do not bother about public opinion. This faith you can get only through experience, not through the intellect.

19 **Q.** Does one see God everywhere and in everything only after reaching the second region or the third region?

A. Even earlier, because you see God's Light and hear His Sound within yourself. Then you start seeing that Light, that Sound, that Creator, in everyone. You start realizing that they are also God's creation and that

God's Light is also in them. This realization starts coming to you even earlier than the second region.

> Q.   Maharaj Ji, God is in everybody, and when a satsangi gets to a certain place he just sees God, God, God. When the satsangi is seeing God, God, God, does he see the world also, this phenomenal world? In other words, the chair I'm sitting on and the sofa—are these things still there as chairs and sofas or are they not seen anymore?

A.   The creation is still there—why not? But he sees the Lord in every part of the creation. The creation is there, it has not vanished. Before that he saw only the creation and not the Creator. Now he also sees the Creator in the creation.

> 20 Q.   Master, will trying to love our brothers and sisters without attachment help us to develop love for the Master?

A.   It is just the reverse. If you are in love with the Master, you will automatically be in love with the brothers and sisters, because then you see the Master in every disciple. You have a common aim, a common objective, a common love, and you strengthen one another's love. But loving one another will not strengthen your love for the Master. If we love the Lord we will all be nearer to one another, because we see the Lord in everyone. But if we love one another, it does not mean that we love the Lord. We may be involved with one another and remain involved just at this level.

Christ said: Remember my two commandments: Love the Lord thy God with all thy heart, and with all thy soul, and with all thy mind. When you are able to attain this level, then he says: Love thy neighbor as thyself.[1] Then the whole universe becomes your neighbor, and you are in love with them as you are in love with the Lord, because you see the Lord everywhere. But the first commandment is essential before you can follow the second commandment.

21 Q. Why is it so difficult for me to make the effort toward spiritual progress?

A. It is always difficult to put in the effort, because we are so attached to this world. We are so much in the habit of putting forth efforts for this world that we find it difficult to put in an effort for Him whom we do not see. Our problem is that what we see does not exist, it is all perishable; what we do not see is real, it is eternal. What we see, we fall in love with, and what we do not see we find it difficult to fall in love with. Without falling in love with the One whom we do not see, we can never escape from this creation. This is the human problem. We always get attached to someone at our own level. We find it very difficult to attach ourselves to someone we have never seen, and that is why we need the living Master.

22 Q. I have heard that a Master after his death cannot appear to anybody other than those who were his direct initiates, but of course Saint Paul saw the image of Christ and had not even met him.[2]

---

1. "Thou shalt love the Lord thy God with all thy heart, and with all thy soul, and with all thy mind. This is the first and great commandment. And the second is like unto it, Thou shalt love thy neighbour as thyself." *(Matt. 22:37–39)*
2. *Acts 22:17–18.*

A. No, a Master can appear to somebody whom he has not initiated. Even now some people who have become satsangis tell me they have seen the Great Master, though the Great Master is no longer here. Many satsangis have told me that they had seen the Great Master before initiation and that they never knew who the gentleman was until they had come here and seen his picture. This is because they may have been his initiates in the past birth.

Q. But this cannot apply to Paul.

A. I do not know about Paul. I am telling you about the statement that when a Master is not here he cannot appear except to those who had an association with him in their past birth. Saint Paul may have had Christ's vision. There is nothing improbable about it, because he may have been Christ's associate in a previous life.

And then Jesus did not leave his disciples orphaned. He appointed Peter to carry on his mission. Every successor walks in the footsteps of his Master because they are all connected with the source. So Paul's own Master, who put him on the path, would have appeared to Paul, and that Master knew Jesus.

23   **Q.** The Bible relates the story of how Jesus took the three apostles—Peter, James, and John—to a high mountain and was transfigured before them, so obviously he must have taken them within. Then Moses and Elijah appeared to them, and the apostles could not take it anymore, and their eyes

became heavy.[1] Now, I thought this might have some special meaning or significance in Sant Mat. It has always puzzled me since I was a child.

A. All that they try to describe is inside. The high mountain indicates that they concentrated their attention within at the eye center. For instance, Moses went to a mountain and he could not bear the thundering Light. That was not outside. That he retired to the mountains for meditation is different, but the thundering Light did not come from anywhere outside.[2] It was within him, but he could not stand it and he fainted.

Q. I realize this, but I wondered what significance this could have, and why Moses and Elijah were brought to this high mountain.

A. Actually it is very difficult to say, because we do not know what was the question of those disciples, what was worrying them, and how the Master wanted to get those things out of their mind. Some disciples are so attached to the previous Masters that unless they see those Masters within, they will never be convinced about the path and will never be able to make progress.

---

1. "And after six days Jesus taketh Peter, James, and John his brother, and bringeth them up into an high mountain apart. And was transfigured before them: and his face did shine as the sun, and his raiment was white as the light. And, behold, there appeared unto them Moses and Elias talking with him." *(Matt. 17:1–3)*

2. "And the angel of the Lord appeared unto him in a flame of fire out of the midst of a bush: and he looked and, behold, the bush burned with fire, and the bush was not consumed" *(Exodus 3:2).*

"And it came to pass on the third day in the morning, that there were thunders and lightnings, and a thick cloud upon the mount, and the voice of the trumpet exceeding loud; so that all the people that was in the camp trembled. . . . And mount Sinai was altogether on a smoke, because the Lord descended upon it in fire: and the smoke thereof ascended as the smoke of a furnace, and the whole mount quaked greatly." *(Exodus 19:16, 18)*

They are so attached to those traditional Masters that sometimes the Master definitely shows the past Masters to them. It does not mean that those Masters come to them, but the disciples may see their forms. The forms may be projected one way or another before those disciples, so that they are convinced that they are on the right path. Then ultimately they rise above attachment to those traditional Masters.

It is just to build faith within the disciples to meditate. So I cannot say from what point of view those visions were before them or what were those disciples' problems at that time and how Christ was trying to help them. Christ makes it very clear that Moses cannot deliver that bread to you now from my Father in heaven: I can deliver the bread to you. He makes it very clear.

> **Q.** Do you think they were still thinking of Moses and Elijah, the past Masters, and this was to get them to accept the living Master?

A. There may have been some problem of those disciples that the Master (Christ) was trying to clear for them, and we cannot analyze these situations because we do not know the background, which does not come in the texts.

> 24 **Q.** There are many people in the Christian world who think they have seen Jesus.

A. It is a projection of their own minds. They have not seen Christ; how do they know what they have seen is Christ? If you judge by the paintings, they differ. Bring together all the paintings of Christ in the world—he is depicted in different colors and different features and in different garments, so how do we know what he actually looked like? It is all the artist's own imagination—what he imagines Christ to be, not what Christ actually was. Christ lived two thousand years ago, and I doubt that we have any painting older than even one thousand years; so how do we fill up that eighteen- or nineteen-hundred-year gap?

Even today, if an artist has seen a model, but if the person is not sitting before him, the artist cannot exactly depict the model. If an artist wants to depict a model whom he has never seen, how can his painting be true to the original? So if somebody meets us inside, how do we know if he is Christ or someone else?

Christ himself explains that inside you meet even Satan. He was met by Satan, who tried to tempt him, but he refused to be tempted![1] It means there are certain powers within that try to deceive us. So how do we know that we are not being deceived within and we are meeting the right Master? That is how we are deceived, unless we use the test given to us at the time of initiation.

> Q. Then is it wrong to even try to see a Master who has passed on many years ago?

A. Some people are so much attached to them that unless they have the vision of the past Mystics, they will not be able to make any progress. So the Master may help them to rise above that in one way or another. But actually it is something very different than really seeing those past Masters.

---

1. *Matt. 4:8–10.*

Whenever you are to see a past Master or any Saint other than your own Master inside, the present Master will bring them along with him, so you will always see them along with your own Master. If they come to you inside otherwise, without your own Master, it means that it is your own mind which is projecting those images to deceive you. As Christ said: Moses cannot deliver that bread to you now, and anyone coming to you inside without me is a robber,[1] because it is your own mind that is projecting that form.

The principle of Sant Mat is that if you want to see a traditional Master and you cannot build faith in your Master without the appearance of a previous Master within, then your Master will bring him within, along with himself, just to create faith in you. Actually, the previous Masters or Saints do not come; it is your own Master who projects them within from the Shabd, or Word.

25 Q. Maharaj Ji, when you said that you are responsible for your Master's sheep, does that mean in the flesh, because surely when his disciples go inside they will see the Radiant Form of their own Master?

A. He will see the form of his Master, no doubt, because he has been initiated by his Master, but the form that he sees is coming out of the Word. The flesh is no more; the Word is the shepherd. The previous Master has taken his form from the Word, and the present Master also takes his form from the Word. The shepherd is one. They may take a different mask. They may

---

1. *John 10:1; 6:32.*

take a different physical body, but that which gives them life is one.

26 Q.   Master, has any Saint in the past ever told his disciples in words who he really is?

A.   Christ said, "I and my Father are one."[1] That is at least what we read in the Bible, but generally Saints do not say such things. It is the disciples who write these things about their Masters; the Saints do not talk. But when reaching to the highest level of consciousness, in their ecstasy, they sometimes say many things to themselves that people hear. But they do not speak to impress people nor for others to hear what they say. They are actually talking to themselves. Mansur exclaimed: I have become God (or something like that). They are not talking to the masses or lecturing to the multitudes. They are just talking to themselves, within themselves, and if anybody hears and writes, that is a different thing.

27 Q.   Christ says: It is expedient for you that I leave you, because as long as I am with you, the Comfortor will not come.[2] Well, you have explained so many times that when the disciple is in the physical presence of the Master, he does not tend to seek the Radiant Form of the Master within. So my question is this: if the disciple is really sincere and works hard even while his Master is alive, can he reach the Radiant Form while the Master is living, or is it possible only when the Master is no more in the world?

---

1. *John 10:30.*
2. *John 16:7.*

A. Oh no! It is easier for us to see the Radiant Form of the Master while the Master is living, provided we follow his teachings implicitly. Then we get practical, direct help. After he leaves this world we can reach his Radiant Form if we attend to meditation, because he has put us on the path. But definitely, we can see him within while he is living and we are living. Christ was really trying to urge his disciples to benefit from his presence while he was still with them.

Q. Maharaj Ji, would you talk about how physical separation from the Master helps in the spiritual progress?

A. It depends upon the individuals. To some it is helpful. For others, if they go out of the Master's presence, they just forget him. It depends upon the individual soul. When you are absolutely in love with the Master and there is physical separation, then probably your pain becomes more intense. But if that longing has not taken root and you go out of the Master's presence, you forget him.

We must have love and devotion for the Master. How it is created—whether by being in his company or by being separated—he knows best. The main idea is to create love and devotion in us. In some people it is created by constant company. In others a little separation is essential. How the Master creates that feeling of love and devotion in us depends upon the individual, but he has to fill us with love and devotion.

Christ also says, near his end: It is expedient for you that I leave, it is in your own interest that I leave now, because my physical body has created that love and devotion in you, but you are still running after me and do not try to seek me within yourself. When you will not find me outside, you will have no option but to turn within, because now you cannot live without me. So that may have been his way of creating love for the Father in them.

Bulleh Shah was forced to stay away from his Master for many years. His Master refused to see him. He said: You cannot see me, you cannot enter my abode. Bulleh was deeply in love with his Master, and his Master wanted to purify him. He knew Bulleh was to succeed him. He wanted to make Bulleh like himself, so in this case the separation was the best way to do that. He knew best; ultimately Bulleh became the Master. Bulleh was the most beloved disciple of his Master, but he was forbidden to enter his Master's courtyard for many years prior to that.

Guru Arjan, the fifth Master in Guru Nanak's line, was sent away by his Master, Guru Ram Das, to Lahore. For many years he was not allowed to come to his Master. Guru Arjan wrote loving and pleading letters to his Master, and his hymns are filled with love, devotion, and longing in separation. It is not that Guru Ram Das did not love him. Guru Ram Das loved him very much, but he wanted to bring him to that level where Guru Arjan could succeed him. So sometimes separation sharpens love.

Until the union, there is always separation in love, and that separation makes us miserable. Even if we meet the beloved, there is always the fear of separation. That fear makes one still more miserable. So until there is complete union, it is very difficult to escape from the misery of separation.

Q. Is there not complete union when we meet the Master inside?

A. Yes. When you become one with the Lord, then there is complete union. As Christ has said, ultimately there is going to be one fold and one shepherd.[1]

28 **Q.** Maharaj Ji, you tell us that we should be happy on the path. Is the pleasure that we find in the separation the cheerfulness you are talking about when you say we should be happy?

A. No. What I mean to say is that under every circumstance one should try to be happy. We have to face everything smilingly, whether it is pleasant or unpleasant. Whatever is in our karma we should face smilingly. Even if we do not face it smilingly, we will have to face it, so why not smilingly?

Q. Maharaj Ji, there is a paradox though. Shouldn't there be a certain serenity, one's walls against the world, so to speak? With time, will serenity come as well?

A. Of course. There is bliss, there is peace, there is serenity within you. People who have no love for the Lord are much more miserable than those who feel the separation from the Father.

29 **Q.** Master, can you explain why Christ changed water into wine?

---

1. *John 10:16.*

A.   These are just myths. The real wine is that Nectar within every one of us at the eye center. That is the real water, the living water that gives us eternal life.[1] It is nowhere outside. What is the sense of going to a Mystic just to change water into wine when we can easily distill wine of our own? It is the spiritual wine that intoxicates us with love and devotion for the Father. *That* wine we get through the Mystics. Not only Christ but also the Persian Mystics have referred to the living water as wine, because wine intoxicates us, makes us forget this world, and spiritual intoxication is the effect of that living water, which takes us to a new world. We forget all our surroundings and we are filled with devotion and love for the Father. Being here, we are not here; we are inside with the Father. That is the effect of this wine.

30 **Q.**   Maharaj Ji, do you agree with Dr. Johnson in what he says in *The Path of the Masters,* more or less, that Jesus Christ was crucified because of the karmas he absorbed due to the miracles that he had performed?

A.   It is very difficult to analyze these things, and I personally think that it is just his personal view. God knows best the reason behind Christ's crucifixion.

   There must have been some divine plan. But for his crucifixion, perhaps we would not have known about Christ today and people would not have benefited by his teachings, because historians always write the history of the people in authority—kings, politicians, generals. If some Mystic comes in conflict with them, he is mentioned, and if they become a disciple of a Mystic, that

---

1. *John 4:10, 13–14.*

Mystic is mentioned. Otherwise, nobody writes the history of a Mystic. Christ came in conflict with the authorities, and his crucifixion is known today to the whole world; so his teachings are also known, and the world has benefited by them. Otherwise he may have just passed on unnoticed. The Lord knows best His divine plan of spreading His teachings—we can only guess why.

It is very unfortunate that we worship the dead and persecute the living. That is the fate of the Saints. We persecute them while they are living and we worship them when they are dead. They are sanctified and treated as God when they are dead, but while they are living we are not even prepared to call them normal human beings. Either we say they are corrupting us or we frame all sorts of charges against them. It happened not only with Christ; it is practically the fate of every Mystic. And now wherever they even sat, we have beautiful memorials; millions and millions of dollars have been spent on them. So we are "wiser" when they die, and we live in darkness and are blind while they are living. That is the pity.

31 **Q.** The whole Christian world, including a member of my family, is convinced that Jesus will come again from the clouds of heaven. You remember the story, that after crucifixion Christ ascended up into heaven in a cloud and receded out of sight.

A. In the Bible Christ has said, I will come again— but that does not mean physically. The Master always comes to the disciple again and again. He says: Now I am in the body, and after a little while you will not see me, but I will come again in my Radiant Form within you.[1]

> **Q.** Yes, I realize that, but now how is it that they all interpret it as a physical event and are convinced that he will return again physically? The whole Christian world believes this.

A. He has not come in the physical form in two thousand years. Even if he comes after another hundred years, of what advantage is it to us? If Christ comes even today, of what advantage is it to the people who have lived and died all through these two thousand years? Supposing they are right, that he comes from the clouds in the same form, of what advantage is it to those who are already dead?

He is referring to his disciples. He is not talking to other people. He prays to the Father: I pray for *them,* not for the whole world.[2] He prays for those whom he has initiated. His whole teaching is for them. He says: For them I will come again—and he may have come a thousand times to them within, although they may have seen him outside also, just as they are seeing a physical body.

> **Q.** So was the ascension actually an internal event? Did his disciples see this within?

A. It was all within. In the Bible they try to explain that Moses saw fire, a red light, in the mountain.[3] That light was not in the mountain, because if so, that light

---

1. *John 16:16.*
2. *John 17:9.*
3. *Exodus 3:2.*

should be there even now. It was within.. He went to the mountain to meditate, but he saw that red light and heard the thundering of the clouds within.[1] And Christ also refers somewhere in the Bible to the lightning and thundering of the clouds. He says that hearing it, people fell flat. They could not bear that Sound and Light within, so they became unconscious.[2] It is nothing physical, nothing outside. It is all within, but those who do not know anything about inner experience interpret all these things as outside events.

Even if Christ has to come again, it means he has to bring his mother, his father, and all his disciples again in the same country and with the same associations. Only then would we recognize him. Otherwise, if Christ came by another mother, how would we know that he had come? And how could that whole drama be repeated again after two thousand years?

32   Q.   Master, I would like to ask one question that has been bothering me. The previous story in Saint John of Christ feeding and eating fish can be explained, but after his crucifixion the disciples forsook him and went to the Sea of Galilee, back to their trade as fishermen, and were without luck. A man was on the bank, according to the story, and he said to cast the net on the other side of the boat. They did, and their nets were filled. Then Christ appeared to them after his crucifixion and ate fish on the edge of the sea. Then, of course, he disappeared.[3] This was his second sort of visionary meeting with his disciples.

---

1. *Exodus 19:16, 18.*
2. *Matt. 17:5–6.*
3. *John 21.*

A. This appearance of Christ after his crucifixion is not something physical. It is his Radiant Form, and when a Master appears in his Radiant Form within the disciple, he won't ask for food to eat. These stories are our way of interpreting things, because except for disciples and seekers, nobody can understand how a man can appear in Radiant Form within. So people have interpreted his inner appearance as being in the physical form outside. If a satsangi says, "I saw the Master here. He helped me; he was with me on my travels," a non-satsangi will naturally think the Master must have been in the physical form. He cannot understand how the Master, a human being, can be in his Radiant Form with the disciple. So that is the interpretation of the people who wrote the Bible later on.

As you know, the Bible was not written in Christ's time, nor by the apostles themselves nor by the people to whom Christ appeared. It was written long after his death. Christ says: I am with you for only a little while, and again I will be with you.[1] Physically, I will not be with you, but spiritually I will be with you again, and you can see me within yourself. So his reference is to something within, not outside. But those who do not understand this interpret it in terms of his physical presence outside.

33   **Q.**   Master, many Westerners believe that eating meat and drinking alcohol has been sanctioned in the Bible, because Christ himself ate fish and fed it to the multitudes and he gave his disciples wine to drink at the last supper. Can you explain this, please?

---

1. *John 16:16.*

A.   Sister, I do not know whether Christ said all this or whether it is only our justification to drink wine or eat fish. It is very difficult to say that Christ allowed his disciples to eat fish or to drink alcohol. I think that after some time, after the demise of Christ, people may have been tempted to take wine and eat fish, and they may have justified it in the Bible. Only then could they be at ease in killing for their palate. Or fish and wine may be symbolic, and in translation it may have been misinterpreted.

[1]In the very first chapter of the Bible you will find that a vegetarian diet is decreed, when you read:

> And God said, Behold, I have given you every
> herb bearing seed, which is upon the face of all
> the earth, and every tree, in which is the fruit of
> a tree yielding seed; to you it shall be for meat.
> And to every beast of the earth, and to every
> fowl of the air, and to every thing that creepeth
> upon the earth, wherein there is life, I have
> given every green herb for meat: and it was so.
> *(Genesis 1:29–30)*

According to the Bible, the word *meat* does not only pertain to flesh, but to food in general.[2] There are other instances in the Bible where flesh meat is disdained, such as:

> But Daniel purposed in his heart that he would
> not defile himself with the portion of the king's

---

1. On going through the manuscript of the present edition, the portion beginning from here and ending with the end of the quotation from the *Essene Gospel of John* has been added to shed more light on the subject.
2. The Hebrew word *le-achlah*, which is translated as "for meat" in the English Bible, does not mean "meat" at all—it means "food."

meat, nor with the wine which he drank:
(Daniel 1:8)

Prove thy servants, I beseech thee, ten days;
and let them give us pulse to eat and water to
drink. *(Daniel 1:12)*

And at the end of ten days their countenances
appeared fairer and fatter in flesh than all the
children which did eat the portion of the king's
meat. *(Daniel 1:15)*

As mentioned in letter No. 441 in *Divine Light,* the
best answer to your question as to whether Christ was a
vegetarian is to quote some extracts from the *Essene
Gospel of John,* sent to me by some satsangis and which
is supposed to be a direct translation from the Aramaic
of the pure, original words of Jesus Christ. I am told that
these ancient and complete manuscripts are in the Vat-
ican Library. You will note that the quotation from
Genesis 1:29–30 is also included in this gospel:

But they answered him: "Whither should we go,
Master, for with you are the words of eternal
life? Tell us, what are the sins we must shun,
that we may never more see disease?"

Jesus answered: "Be it so according to your
faith," and he sat down among them saying: "It
was said to them of old time, 'Honor thy heavenly Father and thy earthly Mother, and do their
commandments, that thy days may be long
upon the earth.' And next afterward was given
this commandment, 'Thou shall not kill!' For
life is given to all by God, and what God has
given, let no man take away. For I tell you truly,
from the Mother proceeds all that lives upon the

earth; therefore, he who kills, kills his brother.
And from him will the earthly Mother turn
away, and will pluck from him her quickening
breasts. And he will be shunned by her angels,
and Satan will have his dwelling in his body.
And the flesh of slain beasts in his body will
become his own tomb. For I tell you truly, he
who kills, kills himself; and he who eats the
flesh of slain beasts, eats of the body of
death. . . . And their death will become his
death. For the wages of sin is death!"

"Kill not, neither eat the flesh of your innocent
prey lest you become the slaves of Satan. For
that is the path of sufferings, and it leads unto
death. But do the will of God that His angels
may serve you on the way of life. Obey, therefore, the words of God: 'Behold, I have given
you every herb bearing seed, which is upon the
face of the earth, and every tree, in which is the
fruit of a tree yielding seed; to you it shall be for
meat. And to every beast of the earth, and to
every fowl of the air, and to everything that
creepeth upon the earth, wherein there is
breath of life, I give every green herb for meat.
Also the milk of everything that moveth and
that liveth upon earth shall be meat for you;
even as the green herb have I given unto them,
so I give their milk unto you. But *flesh and the
blood* which quickens it shall ye not eat!'"

I don't think that Christ would teach that you can eat
fish or drink wine. He says: Whatever you sow, so shall
you reap. So how can he allow killing? He says: Moses
has told you, Thou shalt not kill.[1] What is killing?

---

1. *Exodus 20:13; Deut. 5:17.*

Depriving any creature of its life. Moses never said: Thou shalt not kill humans. He said: Thou shalt not kill.

Christ says: No question of killing—you should not even hurt anybody's feelings.[1] When he was so compassionate and kindhearted, how can you expect him to allow people to eat flesh? How can you expect Christ to kill for food when he does not want to hurt anybody, when he does not want to abuse anybody, when he wants to put his right cheek before you when you slap his left?[2] He is so nonviolent in his approach to everything; how can you expect such a person to kill for his food? He says: If anybody files a suit against you, give everything to him. Do not claim it, even if it is yours.[3] And whatever you give to people, do not fill your pockets in return. Give to them freely.[4] How can we say that such a compassionate, kindhearted, loving person would advise people to kill to eat? How can we think he would be eating meat when he lays so much stress on the commandment of Moses? There is something wrong somewhere in our understanding.

And then Christ tells us: Love thy neighbor.[5] Now, "neighbor" does not mean only human beings. "Neigh-

---

1. "Ye have heard that it was said by them of old time, Thou shalt not kill; and whosoever shall kill shall be in danger of the judgment: But I say unto you, That whosoever is angry with his brother without a cause shall be in danger of the judgment: and whosoever shall say to his brother, Raca, shall be in danger of the council: but whosoever shall say, Thou fool, shall be in danger of hell fire." *(Matt. 5:21–22)*
2. "Ye have heard that it hath been said, An eye for an eye, and a tooth for a tooth: But I say unto you, That ye resist not evil: but whosoever shall smite thee on thy right cheek, turn to him the other also." *(Matt. 5:38–39)*
3. "And if any man will sue thee at the law, and take away thy coat, let him have thy cloke also" *(Matt. 5:40)*.
4. "Freely ye have received, freely give" *(Matt. 10:8)*.
5. "Ye have heard that it hath been said, Thou shalt love thy neighbour, and hate thine enemy. But I say unto you, Love your enemies, bless them that curse you, do good to them that hate you, and pray for them which despitefully use you, and persecute you." *(Matt. 5:43–44)*

bor" means everybody—the birds, the animals, and the humans—around you. You have to love them as you love your own self. Then how can you kill them?

In the Ten Commandments it is very clearly written: Thou shalt nor kill,[1] but after some time we become a victim to these weaknesses and we start justifying them. Either we misinterpret the writings of the Mystics or we wrongly translate them, or in some other way we try to justify our weaknesses.

Buddha was strict about nonviolence. He was a strict vegetarian, but look at what most Buddhists do now—they eat meat and they justify it by saying that they do not buy it, only the servant buys it; that they never ask for it, it only comes before them and they eat it. These are all justifications. You cannot justify these things like that. You cannot fool yourself.

I personally think these teachings did not suit the worldly people in the time of Christ, so they were suppressed or withheld from the masses. Yet there are some schools of thought in Christianity, such as the Seventh Day Adventists, that are vegetarians. They themselves do not know the reason for their being vegetarian but they are vegetarians.

After a lapse of time, we forget the real teachings of the Mystics. We just want to hold on to the shell and lose the reality. We want to hold to traditions, organizations, and do not want to follow the teachings of those Mystics. We think that following the traditions is sufficient, the be-all and end-all. "Buddha is my Master"— that is all. "Jesus is my Master." That is all we want to feel. We do not want to go deep into the reality of their teachings, because they are very difficult to follow. It is

---

1. *Exodus 20:13; Deut. 5:17.*

hard to mold our way of life according to them, so we start compromising with the teachings and go far away from them.

No Mystic will advise you to kill. There should be no contradiction in their sayings. If on the one hand Moses says: Thou shalt not kill, and on the other hand he says: You may eat meat—then how contradictory his sayings become! If on the one hand Christ says: Do not even hurt anybody or even call anybody a fool, and on the other hand he says you may kill right and left for your food—how can you reconcile the two statements? There is something wrong in our understanding.

34 Q. You were saying that Christ told his disciples that once they had gone inside, they would have their questions answered more directly. Is this because they could not understand in their physical form?

A. There are two reasons. The first thing is, our questions outside are worldly. We ask a Mystic for the worldly boons, and all these questions become meaningless when we go to that higher level of consciousness. And Masters never want to interfere in our destiny. Whatever is in store for us, we will get. They may give us strength to face it, but they never try to interfere in our destiny. So they can be evasive to our questions.

The second reason is that we do not have enough faith to follow whatever a Master says, because he seems to be just a human being like us. So Saints will not like to burden the disciple unnecessarily by telling him too much. I mean, they know that the disciple is not going to follow it. He cannot. He has all sorts of doubts.

He wants only the answer which pleases him; he does not want an answer which does not please him.

And inside there are no worldly problems at all, no worldly ambitions, no worldly questions. There the only question is of spiritual progress within, of grace and more grace, of love and more love. What would you ask of the Master inside? What would a lover ask of the beloved when the beloved is before him? "I do not want to lose you! Stay here." That is all that a lover would ask a beloved. He has nothing else to ask and he is getting what he wants. So then there is no question of evading a question.

INDEX

[Italics denote biblical references]

INFORMATION AND BOOKS
ARE AVAILABLE FROM:

The Secretary
Radha Soami Satsang Beas
P.O. Dera Baba Jaimal Singh 143204
District Amritsar, Punjab, India

CANADA
Dr. J. Khanna, 5550 McMaster Road, Vancouver V6T 1J8, B. C.
Mr. Reginald S. Davis, R. R. 1 Crapaud, Prince Edward Island,
COA 1J0

U. S. A.
Mr. Roland G. deVries, 10901 Mill Spring Drive, Nevada City,
Calif. 95959
Col. E. R. Berg, U. S. Air Force (Ret'd.), 4001 Mavelle Drive,
Minneapolis, Minn. 55435
Mr. Roy E. Ricks, 651 Davis Street, Melrose Park, Ill. 60160
Mr. Henry F. Weekley, 2121 N. Ocean Blvd., Apt. 1108E,
Boca Raton, Fla. 33431

MEXICO
Mr. Jorge Angel Santana, Cameta 2821, Jardines Del Bosque,
Guadalajara, Jalisco

SOUTH AMERICA
Dr. Gonzalo Vargas N., P.O. Box 2666, Quito, Ecuador
Mr. Leopoldo Luks, Ave. Maracay, Urb. Las Palmas,
Qta. Luksenburg, Caracas, Venezuela
Mrs. Rajni B. Manglani, % Bhagwan's Store, 18 Water Street,
Georgetown, Guyana

WEST INDIES
Mr. Thakurdas Chatlani, 2A Gittins Avenue, Maraval, Trinidad
Mr. Sean Finnegan, P.O. Box 2314, Port-au-Prince, Haiti
Mr. Bhagwandas Kessaram, % Kiddies Corner, Swant Street,
Bridgetown, Barbados

ENGLAND
Mr. F. E. Wood, % Lloyd's Bank, 20 North Street,
Leatherhead, Surrey

SWEDEN
Mr. T. Gunther, Skakeltorp 6018, 441 00 Alingsas

DENMARK
Ms. Inge Gregersen, Askevenget–15, 2830 Virum

HOLLAND
Mr. Jacob Hofstra, Geulwijk 6, 3831 LM Leusden

WEST GERMANY
Mr. Rudolf Walberg, Falkenstr. 18, D–6232 Bad Soden/Taunus

AUSTRIA
Mr. Hansjorg Hammerer, Sezenweingasse 10, A–5020, Salzburg

SWITZERLAND
Mr. Olivier de Coulon, Route de Lully, 1111 Tolochenaz

FRANCE
Count Pierre de Proyart, 7 Quai Voltaire, 75007 Paris

SPAIN
Mr. H. W. Balani, Balani's International, P.O. Box 486, Malaga

PORTUGAL
Mr. Alberto C. Ferreira, R. Machado dos Santos 20, 2775 Parede

GIBRALTAR
Mr. Arjan M. Thadani, Radha Soami Satsang Beas, P.O. Box 283

ITALY
Mr. Ted Goodman, Via Garigliano 27, Rome 00198

GREECE
Dr. Constantine Siopoulos, Thrakis 7, 145 61 Kifissia

CYPRUS
Mr. Hercules Achilleos, Kyriakou Matsi 18,
Pallouriotissa—T. K. 9077, Nicosia

WEST AFRICA
Mr. Krishin Vaswani, Vaan-Ahn Enterprise Ltd., P.O. Box 507, Monrovia, Liberia

Mr. Nanik N. Balani, Kewalram (Nig.) Ltd., P.O. Box 320, Lagos, Nigeria

EAST AFRICA
Mr. Sylvester Kakooza, P.O. Box 31381, Kampala, Uganda

Mr. Sohan Singh Bharj, P.O. Box 47036, Nairobi, Kenya

Mr. D. N. Pandit, United Timber Traders Ltd., P.O. Box 1963, Dar-es-Salaam, Tanzania

Mr. David Bowskill, P.O. Box 11012, Chingola, Zambia

Mr. Vernon Lowrie, P.O. Box 690, Harare City, Zimbabwe

SOUTH AFRICA
Mr. Sam Busa, P.O. Box 41355, Craighall, Transvaal 2024

Mr. R. Attwell, P.O. Box 5702, Durban 4000

MASCARENE ISLANDS
Mr. D. S. Sumboo, 9 BIS Harris Street, Port Louis, Mauritius.

ISRAEL
Mrs. H. Mandelbaum, P.O. Box 2815, Tel Aviv–61000

U. A. E.
Mr. Jiwatram Lakhiani, P.O. Box 1449, Dubai

KUWAIT
Mr. & Mrs. Ghassan Alghanem, P.O. Box 25549, Safat, Kuwait

AFGHANISTAN
Mr. Manak Singh, % Manaco, P.O. Box 3163, Kabul

SRI LANKA
Mr. D. H. Jiwat, Geekay Ltd., 33 Bankshall Street, Colombo–11

NEW ZEALAND
Mr. Tony Waddicor, P.O. Box 5331, Wellesley St. P.O., Auckland 1

AUSTRALIA
Dr. John Potter, Long Wood Road, Heathfield, South Australia 5153

Mr. A. J. Walker, 8/445, Canning Highway, Melville, Western Australia 6156

INDONESIA
Mr. G. L. Nanwani, Yayasan, Radhasoami Satsang Beas,
   JL. Kelinci Raya No. 32A, Jakarta Pusat
Mr. Odharmal Chotrani, 51 Djl. Bubutan, P.O. Box 144, Surabaya

SINGAPORE
Mr. Bhagwan Asnani, 1806 King's Mansion, Singapore–1543

MALAYSIA
Mr. N. Pal, % Muhibbah Travels Agency, Sdn. Bhd.,
   46 Jalan Tanku Abdul Rahman, Kuala Lumpur 01–07

THAILAND
Mr. Harmahinder Singh Sethi, Sawan Textiles Ltd. Part
   154 Serm Sin Kha, Sampheng, Bangkok—10100

HONG KONG
Mrs. Cami Moss, Hongkong Hilton, G.P.O. Box 42
Mr. Gobind Sabnani, G.P.O. Box 3906

PHILIPPINES
Mr. Kay Sham, P.O. Box 2346 MCC, Makati, Metro Manila

JAPAN
Mr. L. H. Parwani, Radha Soami Satsang Beas, 2–18 Nakajimadori
   1–Chome, Aotani, Fukiai-ku, Kobe–651

*   *   *   *   *   *   *   *

FOR OTHER FOREIGN ORDERS WRITE TO:
Mr. Krishin Babani, Buona Casa Bldg., 2nd Floor, Sir P. M. Road,
   Fort Bombay–400 001, India

Addresses changed since this book was printed:

BOOKS ON THIS SCIENCE

Soami Ji Maharaj
1. *Sar Bachan*

Baba Jaimal Singh
2. *Spiritual Letters* (to Huzur Maharaj Sawan Singh: 1896–1903)

Huzur Maharaj Sawan Singh
3. *Discourses on Sant Mat*
4. *Philosophy of the Masters (Gurmat Sidhant)*, 5 vols. (an encyclopedia on the teachings of the Saints)
5. *My Submission* (introduction to *Philosophy of the Masters*)
6. *Philosophy of the Masters* (abridged)
7. *Tales of the Mystic East* (as narrated in satsangs)
8. *Spiritual Gems* (letters: 1919–1948)
9. *The Dawn of Light* (letters: 1911–1934)

Sardar Bahadur Jagat Singh Maharaj
10. *The Science of the Soul* (discourses and letters: 1948–1951)

Maharaj Charan Singh
11. *Die to Live* (answers to questions on meditation)
12. *Divine Light* (discourses and letters: 1959–1964)
13. *The Path* (first part of *Divine Light*)
14. *Light on Saint Matthew*
15. *Light on Sant Mat* (discourses and letters: 1952–1958)
16. *Quest for Light* (letters: 1965–1971)
17. *Light on Saint John*
18. *Spiritual Discourses*
19. *Spiritual Heritage* (from tape-recorded talks)
20. *The Master Answers* (to audiences in America: 1964)
21. *Thus Saith the Master* (to audiences in America: 1970)
22. *Truth Eternal* (a discourse)

Books about the Masters

1. *Call of the Great Master*—Diwan Daryai Lal Kapur
2. *Heaven On Earth*—Diwan Daryai Lal Kapur
3. *The Living Master*—Katherine Wason
4. *With a Great Master in India*—Dr. Julian P. Johnson
5. *With the Three Masters*, 3 vols.—from the diary of Rai Sahib Munshi Ram

Books on Sant Mat in general

1. *A Soul's Safari*—Netta Pfeifer
2. *In Search of the Way*—Flora E. Wood
3. *Kabir, the Great Mystic*—Isaac A. Ezekiel
4. *Liberation of the Soul*—J. Stanley White, Ph.D.
5. *Message Divine*—Shanti Sethi
6. *Mystic Bible*—Dr. Randolph Stone
7. *Mysticism, the Spiritual Path*, 2 vols.—Prof. Lekh Raj Puri
8. *Radha Soami Teachings*—Prof. Lekh Raj Puri
9. *Ringing Radiance*—Sir Colin Garbett
10. *Sant Mat and the Bible*—Narain Das
11. *Sarmad, Jewish Saint of India*—Isaac A. Ezekiel
12. *Teachings of the Gurus*—Prof. Lekh Raj Puri
13. *The Inner Voice*—Colonel C. W. Sanders
14. *The Mystic Philosophy of Sant Mat*—Peter Fripp
15. *The Path of the Masters*—Dr. Julian P. Johnson
16. *Yoga and the Bible*—Joseph Leeming

Mystics of the East Series

1. *Saint Paltu*—Isaac A. Ezekiel
2. *Saint Namdev, His Life and Teachings*—J. R. Puri and V. K. Sethi
3. *Tulsi Sahib, Saint of Hathras*—J. R. Puri and V. K. Sethi
4. *Tukaram, Saint of Maharashtra*—C. Rajwade
5. *Dadu, the Compassionate Mystic*—K. N. Upadhyaya, Ph.D.
6. *Mira, the Divine Lover*—V. K. Sethi
7. *Guru Ravidas, Life and Teachings*—K. N. Upadhyaya, Ph.D.
8. *Guru Nanak, His Mystic Teachings*—J. R. Puri
9. *Kabir, the Weaver of God's Name*—V. K. Sethi